HOW TO MOVE YOUR BOYF

(and Not Break up with Him)

Are you ready to move in with your boyfriend? Are you even ready to read this book? Complete the checklist below to make sure you're armed with the right supplies (and attitude) to survive the live-in lifestyle.

Relationship Checklist

- ☺ a reliable boyfriend
- ☺ a well-thought-out plan
- ☺ the patience of a saint
- ☺ a case of Advil, and whatever else you use to cope
- ☺ boxes—lots of boxes
- ☺ a trailer, truck, or car with decent trunk space
- ☺ deodorizer
- ☺ bubble wrap and tape gun (preferably one with tape)
- ☺ a best friend ready to pick up the pieces

For Jeremy,
my then boyfriend, now husband.

Ordering
Trade bookstores in the U.S. and Canada please contact:

Publishers Group West
1700 Fourth Street, Berkeley CA 94710
Phone: (800) 788-3123   Fax: (800) 351-5073

Hunter House books are available at bulk discounts for textbook
course adoptions; to qualifying community, health-care, and government
organizations; and for special promotions and fund-raising.
For details please contact:

Special Sales Department
Hunter House Inc., PO Box 2914, Alameda CA 94501-0914
Phone: (510) 865-5282   Fax: (510) 865-4295
E-mail: ordering@hunterhouse.com

Individuals can order our books from most bookstores,
by calling **(800) 266-5592**, or from our website at **www.hunterhouse.com**

HOW TO MOVE IN WITH YOUR BOYFRIEND

(and Not Break Up with Him)

TIFFANY CURRENT

Copyright © 2011 by Tiffany Current

Hunter House Inc., Publishers
PO Box 2914
Alameda CA 94501-0914

Library of Congress Cataloging-in-Publication Data

Current, Tiffany.
How to move in with your boyfriend (and not break up with him) /
Tiffany Current. — 1st ed.

p. cm.
Includes index.
ISBN 978-0-89793-574-6 (pbk.)

1. Unmarried couples. 2. Man-woman relationships. I. Title.
HQ803.5.C87 2011
646.7'7—dc23   2011030440

Project Credits

Cover Design: Brian Dittmar Design, Inc.   Managing Editor: Alexandra Mummery
Book Production: John McKercher   Acquisitions Assistant: Elizabeth Kracht
Illustrations: Jeremy Feig, Brendan Heard   Publicity and Marketing: Sean Harvey
Developmental Editor: Jude Berman   Rights Coordinator: Candace Groskreutz
Copy Editor: Heather Wilcox   Order Fulfillment: Washul Lakdhon
Proofreaders: Erica M. Lee and Jack Duffy   Administrator: Theresa Nelson
Indexer: Candace Hyatt   Computer Support: Peter Eichelberger
Customer Service Manager: Christina Sverdrup
Senior Marketing Associate: Reina Santana
Publisher: Kiran S. Rana

Printed and bound by Bang Printing, Brainerd, Minnesota
Manufactured in the United States of America

9 8 7 6 5 4 3 2 1   First Edition   11 12 13 14 15

❀ Contents

Introduction

*A*fter years of dating the good, the bad, and the very, very ugly, I finally met Jeremy. He was the perfect guy for me. Attractive, but not too attractive. Funny, without being too annoying. Smart, but not intimidating. And nice. An actual nice guy. I couldn't ask for anything more—until one special day he asked me to move in with him. Finally, I would get my happily ever after.

Sure, I had my doubts at first. Moving in together was a big step, but I figured I could handle it. People were doing it all the time, so why couldn't I be one of them? Besides, Jeremy and I had been spending practically every minute together. I assumed living with him wouldn't be *that* different.

Boy, was I wrong.

After one month of cohabitation, I was ready to give up on our relationship, throw his clothes out the window, and "accidentally" leave the front door open so his cat would escape. Yes, our relationship had done a complete 180. Before we moved in together, we were all smiles and steamy glances. After shacking up, we were ready to box it out on pay-per-view.

After one particularly ugly spat, I stormed out of our apartment and phoned a friend. She had the perfect solution to all my problems—Mexican food and mimosas—so I joined her and some of her friends for lunch. After a couple of drinks, I started complaining loudly about my live-in relationship. Why did every conversation with my boyfriend turn into a fight? Why did he find it necessary to leave his dirty socks on every available surface? Why was my live-in relationship hurtling toward the point of no return?

Those "why" questions opened the door to a mass of information. Women left and right started sharing experiences from their own live-in relationships (failed or otherwise). And it turned out that most of them had gone in completely clueless—just like me. Some were able to learn through trial and error, but most of them hit rough patches and ended up calling it quits.

After being bombarded with all their horror stories, I thought one thing: "I wish I had known all this stuff *before* I moved in with my boyfriend." That tiny little thought sent me down the path to writing this book. Surely there were a lot of other people out in live-in relationships (or about to be in them) who had no idea what they were getting into. So why not create a guide to make the transition go a lot smoother?

After months of research, interviews, and dealing with my own personal live-in drama (I'll fill you in on that later),

I wrote *How to Move In with Your Boyfriend (and Not Break Up with Him)*, a book dedicated to the art of the live-in lifestyle. It's fun, factual, and boy-friendly (so feel free to leave it on the coffee table, if you want your boyfriend to pick up some tips). It will help you both figure out where to live, how to split chores, how to share costs, and how to get out of that relationship dry spell (if it ever hits). So sit back and enjoy the read. Even though moving in with your boyfriend is a lot of work, this book will make it a whole lot easier.

1

Shacking Up — Now or Never?

*I*t has finally happened: You're officially done dating. No more creepy guys in bars, no more speed dating of any kind, and no more online suitors who never seem to match their touched-up photos. Why? Because you've finally met *the* guy. The guy who makes your stomach do double back flips (or close to it). The guy who makes you feel like a superstar, whether you're wearing five-inch heels or scruffy slippers.

By now the two of you have settled into the wonderful world of coupledom—commuting across town to each other's apartments, IM'ing naughty messages when you should really be working, and spending countless hours fantasizing about your future together. Life really couldn't be any better. Until, that is, he pops the question:

"Would you like to move in together?"

Wow. Talk about instant gratification. Sure, the first time he uttered "I love you" ranked a ten on your romance-o-meter, but this is even better. He's telling you he wants to spend twenty-four hours a day, seven days a week with you. He wants to share his toothpaste, his toilet paper, and even his TV with you. What a commitment.

But before you jump on the cohabitation bandwagon, read this chapter. It'll help you figure out whether you're ready to shack up now...or maybe never.

◎ The Waiting Period

Once your boyfriend asks you to share his world, the inevitable happens: You begin to fantasize about your new place together. Should you go with the light-blue color scheme or the bright passion-red spread? Should you ditch all your old furniture for something newer, fresher, and more color coordinated? Or should you skip fantasizing, truck down to IKEA, and purchase the Swedish leather sofa of your dreams?

First, *slow down*. Stop thinking about your future drapes and start focusing on whether or not you're actually ready for this step. Sure, you may have been mentally preparing for this moment for years, but that doesn't mean you should jump right into it. Because even though he may be the right guy for you, it may not be the right time in your relationship to move in together.

How do you know for sure? Well, if you're still telling your friends that you're dating the *perfect* guy, then you're not ready to move in with your boyfriend. Because no man—not even

Brad Pitt—is perfect. And if you think your boyfriend is, then you're either delusional or you haven't met the real him.

> **Argument #1**
> "Hey, I've been with my boyfriend for eight weeks, and he's done no wrong. So maybe you're the one who's delusional, not me."

Here's the thing about the first couple months of any relationship—it's what's known as the "courtship" phase (or, as I like to put it, the "I-like-you-so-I'm-not-going-to-scare-you-away-by-acting-like-Gary-Busey" phase). This is the period of time when your boyfriend is on his very best behavior. He really can do no wrong in your eyes, because he's being very careful not to. If you want to know the *real* him, wait until the love mist wears off. That's when you get to see his true colors—the burping,

Courtship Phase   Reality Phase

beer-drinking, scratching-himself-in-inappropriate-places, imperfect colors. This little portion of the relationship is what's known as the "reality" phase.

During this time, you'll discover things you don't like about your boyfriend. In fact, you'll discover things you absolutely hate about him. You may even begin to wonder why you're with him. (And he may wonder the same thing about you.) If the two of you can survive this love/hate phase, then you can handle just about anything. So wait until you pass through this reality check before you even think about cohabitation.

> **Argument #2**
> "Why wait? It's kismet. Besides, I've heard of plenty of people who met, fell in love, and moved in together all in one week's time. If they can do it, then why can't I?"

First, you have to be honest with yourself. Exactly how many times have you *met* those couples who had these one-week whirlwind romances? Sure, your best friend's sister's boyfriend's cousin's basketball coach may have known that couple, but have you ever met the people yourself?

Even if they do exist, you have to keep in mind that they are the exception to the rule. They're kind of like that couple who wins the lottery. Yes, you'd love to be them, but the chance of you having that same luck is about one in three hundred million.

Argument #3
"So what if the odds are against us? I don't care. Love is supposed to be spontaneous."

Skinny-dipping is spontaneous. Streaking is spontaneous. Summer road trips to Las Vegas are spontaneous. But moving in with your boyfriend should *never* be spontaneous. It's a big decision that deserves a lot of thought. If you don't take the time to think it over now, then you may regret it later.

Prime example: Ned from Denver. Ned found the love of his life, Samantha, on a very popular dating website. After a few weeks of the two of them sharing heartfelt e-mails, flirty text messages, and hour-long conversations about the evolution of cats, Ned decided they belonged together—literally. So he quit his job, canceled his lease, and moved his life to the next state over, where Samantha lived. Instead of finding his own place, he moved in with her. Why not? They were meant to be together, right?

Not exactly. After *one day*, Ned figured something out about Samantha: She was crazy. And not the funny, ha-ha, isn't-she-cute crazy. No, she was *psychotic* crazy—mood swings, temper tantrums, and raging bouts of jealousy. She was nothing like the cyber chick he remembered. After giving it their all for a full month, the two of them broke up, and Ned moved back home. But life wasn't easy for him. He had walked away from everything to be with her (his furniture, his friends, his foosball table), so now he had to start all over again.

Live-In Lesson

Take things slow. If this is someone you're meant to spend the rest of your life with, there's no point in rushing it.

If you've only known your boyfriend for a few short months, take the time to get to know him a little better. Find out his deepest, darkest secrets and reveal a few of your own. If you like to eat raw onions, tell him. If you still sleep with stuffed animals, let him know. If you have a weird fascination with *The Muppet Show*, share it with him. Just discover as much as you can about each other. When you're done doing that, test your knowledge with the following quiz.

QUIZ: How Well Do You Know Your Boyfriend?

- When is your boyfriend's birthday?
- What's his last name? Do you know how to pronounce it?
- What does he do for a living? What does he *really* do for a living?
- Does he prefer boxers, briefs, or going commando?
- If he could be any mammal, what would he be?
- Have you ever met his parents? Do they even know you exist?
- Why did his last romantic relationship end? Was it mutual, was it his fault, or was his ex-girlfriend just crazy?
- What's your boyfriend's preferred beverage (coffee, tea, grande caramel macchiato)? How does he take it?
- When your boyfriend talks about the future, are you ever included? Do you want to be?
- If your boyfriend had to live without deodorant or his Xbox, which one would he choose? Would you still love him without deodorant?

Okay, honestly, how many of those questions did you get right? How many of those questions did you completely blank on? Remem-

(cont'd.)

QUIZ (cont'd.)

...ber, relationships aren't just about the big things: They're about the little things, too. If you don't know how your boyfriend takes his coffee, then you haven't been paying attention. If you don't know his birthday, then you two should start talking *immediately*. (If it turns out his birthday was last week, you'd better buy him a gift ASAP.)

Now what about the big things? Maybe you haven't met his parents. This may or may not be a big deal, but that depends on how close your boyfriend is to his family. What about his future goals? If you're planning to move in with him, then you'd better hope his future plans include you. So don't stop asking these questions, and be sure to really get to know each other before you decide to make such a huge commitment. Because you won't just be sharing your closet space—you'll be sharing your life, too.

◎ Bad Habits and Deal Breakers

Bad habits—we all have them. Some of them are silly, such as pushing the toothpaste from the middle of the tube instead of the bottom. Some of them are serious, such as leaving dirty clothes all over the floor. And some of them are severe, such as smoking, heavy drinking, and illegal dog fighting. Either way, bad habits are a big deal, which is exactly why you need to discuss them *before* you and your boyfriend decide to move in together.

Why spill these incredibly embarrassing, potentially disgusting, dirty little secrets before you two share the same digs? Because you want to make sure these habits are something you can *live* with. If they are not, figure out solutions now instead of dealing with the drama later.

Argument #1

"Do I really have to share all my bad habits? What if he freaks out? What if he laughs at me? What if he doesn't want to move in with me?"

Look, your boyfriend isn't going to ditch you just because you hide Milky Way bars in your underwear drawer. Or because you occasionally snack on dog biscuits when you're out of cookies. Yes, he may be surprised to learn these facts about you, but remember that he loves you. If he didn't, then you wouldn't be having this discussion in the first place. So tell him all about your bad habits. He'll be more accepting than you think.

Case in point: my boyfriend's buddy Aaron. Aaron was a little bit of a clean freak. (He was probably born with a bottle of disinfectant in one hand and a paper towel in the other.) But somehow he managed to find a girlfriend who was just as neat as he was. At least that was what he thought—until he randomly dropped by her apartment and discovered a sink full of dirty dishes, clothes strewn all over the place, and a stack of *TV Guides* from the early '90s. Aaron was shocked, not just because she was messy, but because she had kept this secret from him for two years. And in one month's time, they were planning to move in together!

Don't hate me because I'm messy!

Aaron started having second thoughts. If she lied about this, what else did she lie about? Did she really love tofu? Did she really hate punk rock music? Was she really a natural blonde? He didn't know what to believe—until his girlfriend revealed the real reason why she kept her slobbiness a secret. She was afraid that if he knew the truth, he'd not only bail on moving in with her but would bail on their relationship, too. Luckily, the two of them figured out a way to deal with the problem: They hired a maid.

It's your turn now. Be open, be honest, and admit the truth. Make a list of all your bad habits—that's right, even the ones your BFF doesn't know about. If you're still too embarrassed to do it, then take a look at my bad habits to help get you started.

My "Bad Habits" (Personal Habits That May Piss People Off)

1. My hair sheds like crazy, and I never bother cleaning it up.
2. I hog the television on Thursday nights.
3. I read my boyfriend's e-mails when I'm bored.
4. I'm bossy.
5. Sometimes I forget to flush the toilet after I pee.

Okay, some of those items aren't the most appealing habits in the world, but that's okay. Bad habits are supposed to be embarrassing. So take a deep breath, write down all your dirty little habits, and swap lists with your boyfriend. Think of it as a bonding experience—an incredibly weird and awkward bonding experience.

What if you're looking over your boyfriend's list of bad habits (such as nose picking, poor hygiene, cross dressing) and you come across something you don't think you can handle? Well, then you may be looking at a deal breaker, a bad habit you *cannot* live with. Now don't let that statement scare you. You can still work through your deal breakers, but first you have to know what they are. If you're not sure, then think back to former roommate situations (such as your friend, your college bunkmate, or your slutty cousin who stayed with you in the summer of '99) and figure out what you could and could not live with. Those are your deal breakers.

Argument #2
"I don't have to worry about deal breakers. I'm moving in with my boyfriend, *not* a roommate."

Sorry to point out the obvious, but rooming with your boyfriend makes him your *roommate*. Yes, you'll probably be more willing to work things out with him than with your former roomie, but deal breakers are still deal breakers. They will have a *huge* effect on your relationship if you don't recognize them now. So be honest with yourself and your man. It'll make things easier in the long run.

Just look at Jenny from Los Angeles. She was an expert when it came to deal breakers. It wasn't because she had lived with a handful of boyfriends. She'd simply had a dozen different roommates in her lifetime. And after that experience, she discovered what she could and definitely could *not* handle. Her list of deal breakers looked something like this:

Jenny's Deal Breakers

1. No smokers of any kind.
2. Messy people are fine. Dirty people are not. (Believe it or not, there is a difference. Messy means you leave clothes on the floor. Dirty means you leave chicken on the floor.)
3. No party animals. (Partying on the weekend? Okay. Partying every single day of the week? No way.)
4. No wannabe detectives/snoopers.
5. No financially challenged people (that is, people who can't pay their rent on time).

When it came time for Jenny to move in with her boyfriend, she was already prepared. She pulled out her list of deal breakers and discovered that her boyfriend fell into category number five on her list! He was terrible with money. So Jenny had a decision to make. She could either (a) ditch her lovely boyfriend for someone more financially competent and quite possibly boring in bed or (b) work it out. She decided to work it out. When they moved in together, she became the keeper of both their finances so she didn't have to worry about a late rent check and he didn't have to worry about an unhappy girlfriend.

Live-In 🌞 Lesson

Even though one of your boyfriend's bad habits may be one of your deal breakers (or vice versa), you can still find a way to compromise.

◎ **Maybe It's Not Just a Phase**

You've laid it all out on the table. You know his bad habits, and he knows yours. Sure, you may have discovered a few deal breakers along the way, but that's all right. You two have decided to compromise. Now what about the rest of you who have decided you can't? What if you brought up the idea of compromising, and your boyfriend flat-out refused?

Well, you have two choices:

1. Accept his dirty little bad habits (such as thumb sucking, porn addiction, unnatural obsession with Dr. Phil) and learn to live with them.

2. Give him an ultimatum. If he chooses his dirty little bad habits over you, it's time to walk away. Turn down his live-in offer and move on to someone bigger, brighter, and richer or…wait until he gives up this habit and then (only then) start reconsidering whether or not to move in with him.

> ### Argument
> "I'm not doing option 1 or option 2. I'm choosing option 3 — moving in with him anyway — because I know he'll change. This is just a phase. He won't always be like this."

Puberty is a phase. Feathered hair is a phase. Lindsay Lohan's sobriety is a phase. His dirty little bad habits may not be phases. So be honest and ask yourself a couple questions. Have you accepted your boyfriend for who he is? Or do you believe that one day all his bad habits will magically disappear and, suddenly, he'll morph into that perfect specimen of a man? If you're stuck in this mentality, then pinch yourself right now. Better yet, slap yourself, because this type of thinking doesn't help you.

My friend Allison learned this lesson the hard way. After years of dating her boyfriend, the two of them decided to move in together. There was just one tiny hitch—her boyfriend loved smoking a certain illegal substance. He didn't think it was a big deal, but Allison did. Why? Because it was illegal *and* was one of Allison's deal breakers. Instead of talking about it with her boyfriend, she decided to ignore it. She figured it was just a phase. After all, he was turning thirty. It wasn't like he could smoke forever, right?

Well, after a few months of cohabitation, Allison discovered something. Smoking this certain illegal substance was not a phase. *It was his way of life.* Yep, and he intended on continuing this way of life until his lungs gave out. This did not make Allison happy, especially because she had given up her beautiful, rent-controlled, in-close-proximity-to-Trader-Joe's apartment. After trying to learn to live with his bad habit for a few more months, Allison gave up. She broke up with her boyfriend and moved out.

Live-In Lesson

You need to accept your boyfriend for who he is now, not for who he may become in the future.

Let's just say that you've accepted your boyfriend. You love him, want to be with him, and want to have dozens of his babies (if nature permits). But he still has that dirty little bad habit that's number one on your deal-breaker list, and your gut is telling you that maybe this *isn't* a phase. Maybe he's going to do this thing for…*gasp*…forever. Well, if you're not sure, then quiz yourself. Answer all the questions below as honestly as you can, and then accept whatever results you end up with.

✻ ✻ QUIZ: Maybe It's Not a Phase ✻ ✻

1. When you ask your boyfriend about his dirty little habit (such as gambling, drinking, cavorting with strippers), he responds with:
   a. "I only do it when I'm bored."
   b. "I like it. What's the big deal?"
   c. "It's who I am, baby!"

Pick a vice, any vice.

2. How often does your boyfriend indulge in this dirty little habit?
   a. Not often/rarely ever. Maybe once a month.
   b. On a weekly basis.
   c. Three or four times a week. Fine, five times. Okay, six. Is it wrong to say seven?

3. How long has he had this dirty little habit?
   a. He just started.
   b. Maybe a few months—as far as I know.
   c. Years. And years. And…more years.

4. Does he consider this behavior (such as leaving the toilet seat up, picking his toenails, swearing in front of small children) a bad habit?
   a. He knows it's a bad habit, because he told me so himself.

(cont'd.)

QUIZ (cont'd.)

    b. If he does, he's never said anything about it.

    c. Absolutely not. As he puts it, "This is what men do."

5. Does he even realize when he's "doing" this dirty little habit?

    a. He's usually able to catch himself.

    b. Only after I nag him about it.

    c. No, it's just like breathing to him.

6. Does he hide this habit from his family or friends?

    a. No, he has nothing to hide.

    b. Only from a few family members. I've met them. They are judgmental.

    c. There's nothing wrong with keeping secrets!

7. Does he know how much you hate his dirty little habit?

    a. No. If he did, he wouldn't do it as much.

    b. I think so. I did make a few subtle references to it.

    c. I've talked to him about it fifty times. I'm starting to think he's hard of hearing.

8. If you ask your boyfriend if he'll ever give up this dirty little habit, he says:

    a. "Yeah, of course. I'm not going to do this forever."

    b. "I don't know. Why are you pressuring me?"

    c. "No freakin' way. Why would I give up something I love?"

Now count up how many As, Bs, and Cs you have.

Mainly As: You've lucked out! This sounds like it's just a phase he's going through. Basically, it's a hobby that he has for *now*, but most likely it won't be with him for the rest of his life.

(cont'd.)

QUIZ (cont'd.)

Mainly Bs: Hmm, sounds like a middle of the road issue. This is definitely more than a hobby, but he hasn't fully committed to it... *yet*. He could easily go either way, but keep an eye on it. He may make this a regular part of his routine.

Mainly Cs: This is definitely *not a phase*. It's the real deal, so buckle up for a long ride with him and his dirty little bad habit, because this is his way of life.

So how did it go? Pass, fail, or fly off the scale? No matter what, keep in mind that this is just a quiz. Only your boyfriend can tell you whether or not this dirty little bad habit is really just a phase. If he says it isn't, then you have to get real. If his dirty little habit is already causing problems between the two of you, then don't move in together until you've worked things out. Remember, the point of a live-in relationship isn't to *make* something work, it's to take something that's *already* working to the next level.

Chapter Checklist

Keep the following in mind before you shack up:

☐ You're not in a race, you're in a relationship. Don't rush to move in with your boyfriend. Wait until you've really gotten to know each other before you take the live-in leap.

☐ Discuss your bad habits and deal breakers before you decide to move in together. If they overlap, discuss whether you can compromise.

☐ Figure out whether or not that bad habit is just a phase. If it is, you've lucked out! If it isn't, decide whether this behavior is something you want to live with.

2   *Ready, Set...Wait!*

*Y*ou've done it. You and your boyfriend have worked out your potential problems, and you're still here. So treat yourself to a cookie, a facial, or whatever it is that makes you happy, because most people don't make it this far. They run away at the first sign of trouble and never look back. But you're different. You're committed. However, you and your boy toy still have a few steps ahead of you before you take the plunge.

Okay, right about now you're probably rolling your eyes and saying, "I have to do more stuff *before* the move-in? Jeez!" You have every right to be frustrated. In fact, take five minutes to freak out. Put the book down and go scream at a houseplant or some other inanimate object. Whenever you're done, come back and take a hard look at this chapter. It'll help you figure out where your relationship is going, when to plan the big move-in, and how to break the news to your friends and family. (That part may not be pretty.)

◎ Futurama

You're all set for this lovey-dovey, live-in lifestyle, but do you know why you really want to do it? Sure, you're thinking, "Because I love him, silly." Well, yes, that's the obvious answer. You know this. Your boyfriend knows this. Your neighbor down the block knows this (especially if you forget to close the window when you and your boyfriend are...you know). What you need to figure out is the *real* reason why you two are moving in together. Are you doing it to save money? As a way to take your relationship to the next level? Or simply to get away from your sketchy roommate who'd rather spend her time practicing Klingon than speaking English?

Look, people have dozens of reasons to cohabitate (and not all of them lead to a priest, a white dress, and a flock of doves). Who knows, maybe all you want is a long-term, live-in lover with great closet space. That arrangement works for Goldie Hawn and Kurt Russell, and it can work for you, too. So define why you really want to take this leap. Whatever your reason may be, it's totally acceptable.

Once you have your answer, ask your boyfriend why he wants to move in together. And, more importantly, where does he see your relationship going? That's right. It's time to ask your boyfriend about *the future*. (Cue the dark, melodramatic music.) Sure, talking about the future is usually off limits in the world of boys, but this time is different. This is information you must know *before* you two cohabitate.

Argument #1
"Can I be honest? I do *not* want to talk with him about the future. I don't want to scare him off."

Look, if you can't have this conversation with your boyfriend, then maybe you shouldn't be moving in with him in the first place. Instead, prepare yourself for a lifetime of pasta-for-one and taking in stray cats. Because when you're in a live-in relationship, you have to discuss these things, no matter the potential consequences. If you're not ready for a no-holds-barred conversation, slow down. Put off moving in together until you're ready to talk about the future.

But what if you are ready to ask him the biggest question of all questions? How do you go about doing it? Read the following example to help you get started.

Talking about the Future
YOU: "I can't believe we're doing this! You, me, one place. I can't wait. But first, do you mind if I ask you one teensy-

weensy question? I just want to know…where do you see our relationship going?"

HIM: *A look of utter shock and horror followed by an excruciatingly long pause.*

YOU: "Okay, don't freak out. I just want to make sure we're moving in for the same reasons. I'm not asking for a ring or anything—although I do love pink diamonds."

HIM: *A long, relieved sigh.* "Phew. You scared me there for a second. But yeah, sure. Our relationship? I see it going…"

This is a positive example of how "the talk" may end up going. How will it go for you? That depends on your boyfriend (and how good you are in high-pressure situations). Either way, just make sure he knows that you're not trying to force him into anything. You just want to hear his thought process.

Argument #2

"Why bother having this conversation with him? I already know he wants to marry me. If he didn't, then why else would he ask me to move in with him?"

Hmm, maybe because there are a lot of reasons to move in with a person (like you can't afford your rent or you simply want a live-in housekeeper), which is exactly why you should *never* make assumptions. If you disagree, then ask yourself one simple question: Are you a mindreader? Because a lot of women out there think they are. Don't deny it. You've probably thought the same thing at some point in your life. Some guy gives you a look, a wink, a half-smile, and you think, "Yeah, he wants me." But in reality, he doesn't. You just happened to be in his line of vision when he was thinking about last night's game or a thin-crust pizza. So stop thinking you can read minds. You can't.

It took Bianca, a former live-in relationshipper, a long time to figure this out. Why? Because she had a superhero complex when it came to her boyfriend. She always thought she knew exactly what he was thinking. So when he asked her to move in with him, she assumed it was for one reason—he wanted to marry her. She was ecstatic...so ecstatic that she didn't bother asking him if that actually *was* his reason. Once the two of them moved in together, Bianca started making a timeline in her head that looked something like this:

1. In six months, he'll propose.

2. In twelve months, we'll get married.

3. In fifteen months, we'll buy a beautiful little cottage together on the Vermont coastline.

4. In forty-eight months, we'll have kids, twins—Sherry and Perry—who will both grow up to be chemical engineers.

So what happened with Bianca's plan? Six months after they moved in together, no proposal occurred. No biggie— she figured he just had cold feet. Months later, still nothing. After one whole year of living together, Bianca finally brought up the subject of marriage. To her surprise, she learned he had no intention of proposing any time soon. In fact, he had no intention of getting married, period. He had thought they were moving in together to save money.

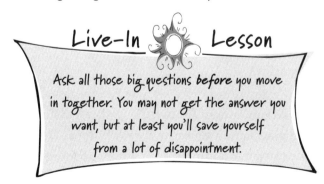

Live-In Lesson

Ask all those big questions *before* you move in together. You may not get the answer you want, but at least you'll save yourself from a lot of disappointment.

Let's say you two have the talk and decide to move in together as a trial before marriage. Great! Now come up with a timeline. Because even though you and your boyfriend see this live-in relationship as the first step toward marriage, you may not see it happening in the same amount of time.

This doesn't mean you should write out a marriage timeline, sign your blood on the dotted line, and say, "Or else." A timeline isn't that rigid (or that morbid, either). It's just a guideline to keep you on track and satisfied with your live-in relationship.

So what do you want? To live together for two years, and then have that unforgettable destination wedding of your dreams? Preferably in Bora Bora (if the weather permits)? What about your boyfriend? Does he want to wait two years before taking the marriage plunge—or is he hoping to wait even longer? If so, is that something you can deal with? If not, try to compromise. Come up with a schedule that you can both agree on.

◎ Pick a Date

By now you and your boyfriend have had the talk. The good news is you survived it. You're still together, laughing, smiling, and putting up with each other's nonsense. Now comes the easiest step in the moving in process—deciding on a date, the *perfect* time to move in together. That's right. So instead of rushing to combine your towels, your throw pillows, and your *Buffy* DVDs without a second thought, you have to sit down and figure out a move-in date that works for both of you.

> **Argument**
> "You want the two of us to talk again? Forget it. The hard part is over. Moving in is easy."

Actually, moving in is not easy. Moving is one of the hardest things you'll do in your life (next to getting into med school and finding the perfect pair of jeans that doesn't make your butt look big). Moving includes a lot to take care of: getting rid of furniture, hiring movers, fighting with uncooperative packing tape, and transferring utility bills. It's a slow, wretched, tedious process. So do yourself a favor and choose a day that's good for you. It doesn't have to be three months from now. It doesn't even have to be three weeks from now. If next weekend looks good, then go for it. But first, make sure to follow one itsy-bitsy rule when selecting a date:

**Avoid moving in together
during a stressful time in your life.**

That's right. If Christmas, Hanukkah, Arbor Day, or any other important occasion is right around the corner, you may want to hold off for a bit. Generally, your budget is pretty tight around the holidays, so wait until afterward before you make the big move. If you have a serious project you have to spend all your time working on, now may not be the best time to move either. Moving is stressful enough. Why do it at a time when you're already overloaded?

Lori, from Nashville, learned about this move-in stress the hard way. After three blissful years of dating her boyfriend, the two of them finally decided to bite the bullet and move in together. Because they'd been together for years, Lori figured that it would be a breeze. Their lives were already intertwined, so moving in a few boxes here or there wouldn't be that hard.

Or so she thought.

Choose wisely.

Unfortunately, Lori's boyfriend picked the worst time ever to move in—right before her LSATs. Whenever Lori tried to study, her boyfriend would take that opportunity to tear open boxes, to move furniture around, or to nail weird paintings onto the wall. Lori was pissed, not just because of her boyfriend's bad taste, but because he was making it impossible for her to study. After venting at him for a few minutes (and practicing a little Ashtanga yoga), she realized that he and his awful art weren't the problem. They had simply picked the wrong time to move in together.

So look at your calendar and pick out a date that works for both of you. When you're done, compare it to the list below to make sure that day will be as stress-free as possible.

The "Not-the-Best-Time-for-a-Move-In" List

Are you and your boyfriend moving in together the same weekend that:

1. your ten-year high-school reunion is happening? (You're cranky from trying to lose those fifteen extra pounds.)

2. you're in heavy training for a marathon, a triathlon, or a high-stakes limbo competition?

3. you have a midterm, a final, a school project, a quarterly report for work, or any kind of standardized test?

4. you're a bridesmaid in your sister's wedding? She expects you to be in top form to catch the bouquet.

5. Nordstrom is having its half-year sale?

Are any of these big events coming up? If so, then you may want to reconsider the move-in date. Why? Because your niece only has one first birthday, your Great-Aunt Sue only comes to town once a year, and you only get one shot to be a contestant on *The Price Is Right*. So if these big events don't happen every day, why would you plan your move-in date around the same time? Do yourself a favor. Pick a date that makes sense.

🌀 Playing Telephone

Now comes the interesting part—telling your family and friends about your big decision. And yes, you are obligated to tell the people you love that you're moving in with your boyfriend. They need to feel as though they're still being included in your life. Besides, after you two move in together and things start to go wrong (and they will), you're going to need the moral support.

Who should you tell first? For most of you, the first branch on the telephone tree will be your friends. They know your boyfriend and know he's relatively normal, so they should be supportive, right? Besides, some of them have been through their own live-in relationships. Sure, maybe some of their relationships didn't work out, but that doesn't mean your friends won't be supportive now.

Wrong. Unfortunately, sometimes our friends—even our BFFs—can be our biggest critics. So prepare yourself for the worst. Better yet, take a look at the potential responses you may hear when you finally break the news.

What Your Friends May Say When You Break the News

1. Live-in relationships never work out.

2. If you wanted a roommate, you should've just asked me.

3. I didn't think you guys were *that* serious.

4. At least this way you'll realize he's not right for you.

5. Enjoy it while it lasts.

Argument
"Umm...no. My friends would never say that to me. They love my boyfriend."

I used to think the same thing when I moved in with my boyfriend. I figured my friends would be happy for me and buy me gifts, or at least a few celebratory drinks.

But that little fantasy ended after I told one person my big news. Her response: "I'll give it six months." And she actually kept track! After each month I lived with my boyfriend, she'd count down: "Five months left until you two break up. Four months. Three...two...." It was not encouraging.

So get ready for a little negativity. Because even though your friends' comments may be harsh, they won't compare to what your relatives may say when you break the news.

What Your Relatives May Say When You Break the News

1. You're too young. (That one depends on your age.)

2. You hardly know this guy. He could be a murderer or a serial rapist. Don't you watch the news?!

3. He's never going to marry you now.

4. Your grandmother would be rolling over in her grave if she knew.

5. You saw what happened to your sister when she moved in with her boyfriend. What makes you think that you're any different?

Ouch. Not exactly the type of thing you want to hear. And most likely when you do hear these comments, you'll want to say something like, "How could you say that to me when I supported you when you (insert a stupid decision), and (insert an even more stupid decision), and even (insert a decision that's so stupid it shouldn't even be mentioned, but you're so pissed that you'll mention it anyway)?!"

Okay, don't go there. You don't want to turn this into an episode of *Jerry Springer* and have your extensions pulled out for no reason. In reality, your friends and family don't want your relationship to fail. They're just afraid. In your friends' cases, they're afraid that you'll disappear into the world of coupledom and never be heard from again. Your family is afraid that you're making a mistake. It's not because they don't trust you. They just still think of you as a little kid, so they're not sure if you're ready to make this kind of decision. But now that you know what the problem really is, there's one thing you can do to curb their fears. Simply say:

> *"I'm sorry you feel that way, but I've already made my decision, and I'm sticking to it. But I would love to hear any advice you have to offer."*

That's it. That's all you have to say, because you're letting that friend or disapproving parent know that you're committed to this decision *and* want the person's help in making this live-in relationship a success. By asking for advice, you're admitting that this isn't just scary for them but scary for you, too. And this way they'll know that you still want and need their support, no matter what their opinions are. So be open about your move-in news. Yes, you may hear a lot of negative responses, but you may hear a few positive ones, too. Either way, you want the people who matter the most to be informed about your life—regardless of whether or not they approve of it.

Chapter Checklist

Review these guidelines before taking the plunge:

- ☐ Discuss the real reason why you're moving in with your boyfriend. (If this sounds scary, find a way to relax first: have a glass of wine, soak in a hot tub, whatever works for you.)

- ☐ If you're moving in together as a trial run before marriage, set a general timeline for when you and he would like those wedding bells to ring.

- ☐ Decide when you two should move in together. Pick a date that works for both of you.

- ☐ Tell your family and friends that you're moving in with your boyfriend. Prepare yourself for the worst response. And remember, no matter what they say, you can always ignore it.

3

My Place or Yours?

*Y*ou're all set. You've followed the precautions, you've taken the mini-quizzes, and you've even phoned a friend about the news. As a matter of fact, you've already circled some apartment ads in the newspaper and bookmarked a few rental places online. Why? Because you're ready for the fun stage—the moving-in stage.

But before you rent that moving van, you need to discuss a few more things with your boyfriend. Namely, where are you going to live—his place or yours? Do you want to get a new place together? If so, do you know what you want/need from your next apartment? If you've already answered these questions, you can skip forward to Chapter 4. If you haven't, then sit down, relax, and take your time with this chapter. You may discover a few options that you never even knew existed.

◎ Trial and Error

One option is to *not* get a new place together. That's right. Sometimes the best way to begin a live-in relationship is to stick with the basics, so start with what you already have. Instead of finding a new place, move into your boyfriend's apartment or let him move into yours. This way you can have a trial live-in situation for a few months before you get a new place together.

Argument #1

"Let me make sure I'm hearing you right. I read through two chapters of your book for you to tell me not to get a new place with my boyfriend? How do I get a refund?"

You're already making a life-changing decision, so you don't need to change your life more than you have to. Make sure that this live-in situation has a fighting chance before you give up everything in your name. See, that's the thing about moving in together. Inevitably, you'll have to go through your collective stuff, junk some of it, or get brand-new things in order to mesh your lives together. So instead of you *both* giving up your apartments and then realizing two months down the line that cohabitation doesn't work, do a trial run first.

If you're not completely sold on that logic, think of it in terms of buying a new car. You never walk into a dealership and say, "Give me that one!" without test driving the car first. Why? Because even though it's pretty and shiny and smells really nice, you want to make sure that you're comfortable in it. So you take it around the block a few times, test out the gear shifts, and make sure you actually like driving it. After you're done doing that *and* weighing the pros and cons, then you decide whether or not this car is for you.

> **Argument #2**
> "You can return a car if you don't like it. If our live-in doesn't work out (which would never happen), then we'll just give up our new apartment. No biggie."

Actually it *is* a biggie, because whenever you rent an apartment, you have to sign a lease. A lease is a binding *legal* document. It holds you to staying in that particular apartment and paying the rent there for a certain number of months (or years). So if you and your boyfriend break up and the lease is still active, your living situation could get very awkward, very fast.

My friend Yvonne had the honor of experiencing that awkwardness firsthand. She moved in with her boyfriend after dating for a year and a half. They were in love. They were happy. And they both wanted the same things: a white picket fence, matching 401(k)s, and a Yorkshire terrier named Noodles. So they took the plunge, gave up their apartments, and moved into a nice, new, two-bedroom place just a few blocks from Saks Fifth Avenue.

After a mere three weeks, Yvonne was over it and over him. Why? Because her boyfriend had turned into the roommate from hell. He refused to do any chores, had his friends over until 2:00 AM every night, and always deleted *Grey's Anatomy* from the DVR. If life was this bad just *living* with her boyfriend, then what would it be like when they were married? Yvonne didn't want to find out, so the two of them broke up.

One problem—they signed a one-year lease, and they could not get out

Is it too late to get my deposit back?

of it! So the two of them (ex-boyfriend and ex-girlfriend) were forced to live together for the next eleven months. It was not a pretty situation, but luckily they had a two-bedroom apartment. At least that way they could easily escape each other, although it was still uncomfortable, especially when her ex-boyfriend wanted to bring his *new* girlfriend over to their apartment.

Live-In ❀ Lesson

Try living together first (at his place or yours) before you sign a new lease together.

Don't be ashamed of wanting a trial-and-error period. There's nothing wrong with testing out your live-in to see if the situation is right for you. If you can afford it, keep both your apartments during the test run. If you can't, then it's time to figure out which apartment to share and which one to give up.

Sure, your first inclination will be to say, "Mine. Stay at my place. It's better than his!" That's probably true. You probably do have a fabulous apartment with a fabulous view of the park and a fabulous walk-in closet that makes your friends drool with envy. But that doesn't matter anymore. Now you have to be realistic about what suits you *and* your boyfriend. So take a look at the following guidelines to help you figure out whose place gets the final seal of approval.

His Place or Yours Guidelines

Proximity to attractions. Whose place is nearest to what you truly need (such as the grocery store, movie theaters, or a Six Flags amusement park)? If your place is in the middle of nowhere and his place is in the middle of somewhere, choose somewhere.

Closest to work. If your beau's place is an hour away from where you work and yours is only five minutes away, you have an easy choice. But how far away is it from his job? Which place is the best compromise for commuting?

Size. Yes, size truly does matter. If he's living in some three-hundred-square-foot bachelor apartment with a combination kitchen/bathroom/closet and you have a lovely one-bedroom pad, then c'mon, tell him to be realistic. You need to make sure your shared apartment is big enough for both of you.

Cost (aka money, money, money). It always comes back to money. If he has a wonderful, rent-controlled apartment and your place is bleeding you dry, then give it up. Saving money is a good thing. (And you can spend the extra cash on shoes.)

Pet-friendly. If you have a pet and his apartment doesn't allow them, well, then the decision has been made for you. You're staying put, and he's moving into your place (unless you're willing to give up your pet Frou Frou).

Keep in mind that this isn't a "must" list. It's just something to help get you started with your own set of guidelines. Maybe other things are important to you, such as access to public transportation, the safety and quality of the neighborhood, or proximity to a sushi bar. That's fine. Just come up with a list of items that are important to you and your boyfriend.

> Argument #3
> "Okay, these guidelines are great and all, but what if I don't want to give up my place? After all, if we break up, I'm the one who'll be homeless."

Live-in relationships are a crapshoot. You always have a chance of ending up apartment-less and boyfriend-less and crashing on your best friend's couch for the next three months (if she'll have you). If you don't want to take that chance, maybe it's time to rethink shacking up altogether. But if you're feeling ready for that next step, give it a shot. It's not called a leap of faith for nothing.

☺ Thinking Short Term

Some of you don't want to take the "his place" or "her place" route. Maybe you already have a roommate, so your apartment is not an option. Or maybe you have a crappy landlord. Or maybe you've seen too many seasons of *Extreme Makeover: Home Edition*, and you're ready to unleash your inner interior decorator on a new place of your own. Either way, if you feel you *have* to test out your live-in in a new apartment, then go for it. But just make sure to follow two big guidelines.

Guideline #1: Find an apartment with a short-term lease. This really is vital, because the first couple months of any live-in relationship are the trial period. This is when you begin to have doubts and to ponder such issues as, "I love him, but can I really live with his man funk?" or "Maybe I should've just gotten a cat." So if you absolutely *must* get a new place together, be smart about it. Find something for the short term.

Start by looking for places that rent on a month-to-month or three-month basis. If you can't find one, then go for a six-month lease. Just try to stay away from signing anything long term. If living together doesn't work out, at least you'll have an end in sight that you can deal with.

If you're having trouble finding a short-term lease, check out sublets. Plenty of renters out there are dying for someone to take over their leases. (Most likely these are unhappy couples who didn't follow my guidelines. You know who you are.) And if you're lucky, once the original lease runs out, you'll be able to negotiate a month-to-month lease from that point on.

Argument
"What if I can't find a short-term lease? What if the only apartments I like have one-year leases?"

Whenever you can, take the short-term lease over the long-term lease. But if you do happen to find the apartment of your dreams with a long-term lease, then go for it. Ultimately, you should do what makes you and your boyfriend happy. Just find out a few details from your future landlord first: Has anyone ever sublet an apartment in the building before? Is it even allowed? (This could be a good "out clause" in case your cohabitation doesn't work out for the better.) Make sure to find out all this information *before* you sign the lease.

Guideline #2: Look for your new apartment together.
Finding a new apartment is a joint venture, so both parties should take equal time looking for it. Don't let your boyfriend tell you otherwise. If you hear him utter the words, "But, baby, I don't know anything about apartment hunting. You do it. You know what I like. I trust you," *do not fall for it*. Why not?

Because I fell for it.

Years ago (before I was an experienced cohabitant), my boyfriend and I decided to look for a new apartment together. I was superexcited, and he...well, he didn't want to be bothered with the process, so he told me to find a place myself. So I spent weeks—months, even—researching apartments, looking for the one in the right location, for the right price, with the right amount of natural sunlight. Then one day I found it, *the* perfect apartment—the kind of apartment you see on television and think, "There's no way that exists." But it did! I showed my boyfriend our future new place and, after giving it the once over, he said, "Why would I ever want to live *here*?"

Our relationship almost ended that day. There was a lot of yelling, a lot of fighting, a lot of, "But you told me to find a place on my own!" Eventually, I calmed down and realized the biggest mistake I made was believing he was being honest when he said, "I don't care where I live." Because he did care—he was just being lazy.

Live-In Lesson

Your apartment is for both of you, so you both need to take the time to look for a new place together.

How can you avoid the same mistake? Come up with a list of what you *need* and what you *want* in an apartment. Not sure of the difference? Then take a look at this example:

Your Apartment "Wants"

- ❀ a dishwasher
- ❀ paid utilities
- ❀ a gold-plated Jacuzzi
- ❀ a balcony overlooking the ocean
- ❀ a kitchen that smells like chocolate

Your Apartment "Needs"

- ❀ a refrigerator

- ⑧ central heating/air
- ⑧ rent control
- ⑧ pet friendliness
- ⑧ a parking spot

Make sure your boyfriend makes a list of his own, and then compare and contrast. If one of your wants or needs is missing from your boyfriend's list (or vice versa), simply combine both lists to make sure you find an apartment you both can live with—or rather, live *in*.

◎ In Escrow

Maybe you've decided that you don't want to move into your boyfriend's place. And maybe he doesn't want to move into yours. Maybe you'd both rather put your rent money toward a condo or a starter home with a koi-filled pond. After all, you two are meant to be together. So why not skip the rental process and just buy something together?

If you're not married or in some form of a legal partnership, this is a *bad* idea. Actually, it's a terrible idea. (Seriously, have you been paying attention?) If you haven't taken the time to make sure that your live-in works, then *do not* go down this path. Yes, buying a house with your boyfriend may make sense when it comes to your finances, but it could really hurt you in the long run.

> ### Argument #1
> "Not true. If we buy a place together, then the stakes are higher. It proves we're really committed to our relationship."

That was exactly what Jennifer Aniston and Vince Vaughn thought in the movie *The Break-Up*. They were so much in love that they bought a condo together without having any type of legal agreement in place. What happened? After dealing with each other's bad habits, terrible decorating taste, and kooky family members, they broke up. They ended up selling the condo (probably at a loss) and being incredibly unhappy about it.

Live-In ✹ Lesson

Having higher stakes doesn't mean you're more serious about your relationship. It simply means you have more to lose.

What happens if you survive the trial live-in period and you still want to buy property together? Well, if you're married, then go for it. But if you aren't, be smart about it. You two are combining your assets to buy a home together, so make sure you have a legal agreement in place before you do it.

> **Argument #2**
> "A legal agreement? Seriously? How's that romantic?"

Love letters are romantic. Moonlight walks on the beach are romantic. Matthew McConaughey movies are romantic. Buying a home isn't supposed to be romantic. You're dealing with a lot of money, so you need to be careful with it. If for some reason you find yourself in an alternate universe where you and your boyfriend —*gasp*— break up, you need to make sure you'll be prepared. Discuss what will happen to your property if your relationship doesn't go as planned.

Here are some questions you should ask during this discussion: What will happen to your townhouse, yacht, McMansion, or whatever if your relationship ends? Will you sell it and split the profits? Will one of you keep the place and pay the other one off? What about the furniture you bought together? How will you split this up? And who gets the Peanuts' figurine collection? Take the time to discuss these details ahead of time. And put whatever you come up with in writing.

Once you've figured all this out, have a lawyer write up a legal document or create one yourself. Generally you can find a sample prenup-type agreement online. (Google is a godsend.) Change the items as needed, sign it, have it notarized, and make sure you each keep a copy for yourself. Ta-da, the end, you're done. That's not so hard now, is it?

What if one of you already owns your own place? Then what? Simply follow the same logic. If your boyfriend is moving into your home and you still have a mortgage, figure out who pays for what. Is he going to pay more, less, or the same amount for the mortgage? Once that's decided, you need to write up a sample lease. Yes, a *lease*. If this is your home, make sure you have a legal document stating your boyfriend does not have a stake in your property.

This may seem a little overly cautious, but it really isn't. This is your home. The place you spent days, weeks, and months researching to find. You saved your pennies and even cut back on your daily Starbucks allowance to buy this place, so there's nothing wrong with protecting it. That doesn't mean you love your boyfriend any less. You're simply protecting your assets, because there's nothing romantic about becoming homeless.

Chapter Checklist

Don't rent that moving van until you review these tips:

☐ Instead of finding a new place together, move into your boyfriend's apartment or let him move into yours. (And if you move into his, make sure to bring air freshener. Lots of air freshener.)

☐ If you have to get a new apartment, find one with a short-term lease or look into sublets.

☐ Do not buy property together. If doing so is unavoidable, write up a legal document outlining what will happen if your relationship ends. (And no, a Post-it does not count as a legally binding document.)

4

Splitsville...
the Good Kind

*M*oney. Yes, good, old-fashioned money. People love having it but hate talking about it. Talking about money is boring and icky and makes you feel downright dirty (like how you feel after watching a Dane Cook movie). So if money talk makes you queasy, by all means skip ahead to the next chapter. Don't worry, no one will judge you. Just as long as you come back and read this chapter later.

Money can make or break your live-in relationship, which is why you and your boyfriend need to talk about it before you move into your new digs. So grab a pen and prepare to take notes. This chapter will help you figure out everything you and your boyfriend need to know about each other's finances. Let the money talk begin!

◎ Money Talks

It's time for you and your boyfriend to get really honest with each other. (And no, that doesn't mean you should tell him how much you hate that grimy red shirt of his, even though it's clearly awful.) The two of you need to get real about your money—how much you have, how much you spend on a monthly basis, and how much you owe.

A penny for your thoughts?

Why are you doing this? Because you two are combining your lives, which means you'll be sharing the responsibility when it comes to bills. Before you decide who pays for what (and what you can even afford), you need to know how much you both *have*. That thought alone may be a little cringe-worthy, but it has to be done. You need to know each other's total income before you can determine how to handle your expenses. How do you do this?

Step #1: Admit the truth.

Let's say you go first. Tell your boyfriend how much you really make per year. Sounds scary, doesn't it? Your boy toy is about to find out how little you make. Or, worse, he's going to find out that you make *a lot* more money than he does. If you want to freak out right now, go for it. Scream at the top of your lungs, jump in your neighbor's pool, down three boxes of snack cakes. Get out the anxiety now so you can let the truth out later.

Once you've calmed down, reveal your income to your boyfriend and ask him to do the same. For some of you, this conversation will go over smoothly. For others, it may play out like this:

YOU: "So... I make X amount of money per year." *Phew. You sigh, relieved that it's over.*

HIM: "Good for you. I would tell you how much money I make, but it's not necessary. Why don't we just split everything fifty-fifty?"

His response is what's known as "resistance." Do not let him get away with this little ploy, because splitting things fifty-fifty may not be the right solution for you. You'll never know unless you have some idea what you both earn and owe on a monthly basis. So calm your boyfriend's nerves. Let him know that you're not planning on knocking him off for his money (or his PlayStation). You just want to know about his finances so you can split your expenses accordingly.

Still not sure if you can hold strong during the "money talks" conversation? Take the quiz below to see if you need a refresher.

✳   ✳   ✳   QUIZ: Money Talks   ✳   ✳   ✳

You sit your boyfriend down to talk about your salaries. After you dish on your income, he says, "Wow, good for you, honey. I wish I could tell you what I make, but I don't know. Everything's direct deposit, so I really have no clue." Do you respond with:

1. "Oh, that's okay. Don't worry about it."

(cont'd.)

QUIZ (cont'd.)

2. "I guess we can just split everything fifty-fifty. Maybe you could check into that later?"

3. "Direct deposit, huh? Well, I guess that means you'll have to check your bank statement. Or better yet, call up HR at your job and ask how much you make. Here, use my phone."

The correct answer is option "3." Call your boyfriend out on any lies or excuses he gives you for not *knowing* his salary. Too many resources are available to help him figure it out. And if he genuinely doesn't know how much money he makes, well, that's just sad.

Step #2: Discuss your debt and your monthly expenses.
That's right. You two need to share all your business. He needs to know about your student loans (if you have any), your monthly minimum on your credit card (don't pretend like you don't have debt), and all your other monthly bills. And you need the lowdown on his car payment, cell-phone bill, gym-membership fee, and fruit-of-the-month-club subscription. So share all this information with each other. Then make a list of every bill you have to pay on a monthly basis and how much it costs you.

Step #3: Discuss your credit.
No, not credit cards, you've already done that. You need to find out what kind of credit your boyfriend has. Whether

it's good, bad, or uglier than your neighbor's baby, his credit score (and yours) will determine a lot of factors in your live-in lifestyle. How so? If your credit score is low, you may not be able to get that great apartment you wanted. If you have bad credit, you may have to pay deposits when setting up your utility bills. So get the facts now, because you need to know what you're getting yourself into.

◎ Splitting Costs

The secret's out—how much you make and how much you owe. Was that so painful? Now all you have to do is figure out how you and your boyfriend will split your expenses.

> **Argument #1**
> "Forget it. I'm done. I've already done the hard part—deciding to move in with him. All that money stuff will work itself out on its own."

This is your money you're talking about. Money determines how you live on a day-to-day basis. If you just throw your money in the air and hope for the best, don't be surprised when a huge gust of wind blows it out of reach. You can't be reckless with your money, especially when you're sharing expenses with another person. So work everything out beforehand. If you don't, it may cause more problems than you think.

A prime example is Katie, a former live-in relationship gal who used the pay-as-you-go logic. How did that work exactly? Well, Katie and her boyfriend's philosophy was whoever had the money at the moment paid for everything. That's how it went for a few months, until Katie found herself forking over the majority of the money. Because whenever rent time rolled around, her boyfriend always claimed he was too broke to pitch in. In all reality, he was just blowing his paycheck on beer and online poker, because he knew that Katie would pick up the slack.

Don't let this to happen to you. Do yourself a favor and work out a few details. If you don't want to take the time to calculate exactly who should pay for what, then a simple solution would be to split things fifty-fifty. Just create a list of all your shared living expenses, calculate the total, and divide it by two. As Michael Jackson would say, it's as "easy as 1, 2, 3." Just check out the example below:

Our Shared Monthly Expenses

```
$1,300  rent
  +$25  renter's insurance
  +$40  utilities
  +$75  phone bill
```

```
+$200   live-in masseuse
+$100   cable TV/satellite bill
 +$30   Internet connection bill
+$200   groceries (for the month)
 +$30   repairs/home maintenance/other
```

```
$2,000   our shared monthly expenses
```

Once you have your shared monthly expenses, divide that number by two. The result equals your portion of the shared monthly expenses.

Here's a sample equation:

My Portion of the Shared Monthly Expenses

```
$2,000   our shared monthly expenses
   ÷ 2
```

```
$1,000   my portion of our shared monthly expenses
```

Voilà. You're done. See, math can be simple *and* fun. (Okay, maybe "fun" is an exaggeration, but you get the point.) Now let's go one step further. Take your portion of the shared monthly expenses and add that number to your own personal monthly expenses (such as, credit card bill, student loans, and red hair dye #5). The total equals how much money you owe/spend on a monthly basis. For example:

My Total Monthly Expenses

```
  $1,000   my portion of the shared monthly expenses
+ $500    my personal monthly expenses
```

```
  $1,500   my total monthly expenses
```

You're figuring out your total monthly expenses for a reason. (And no, it's not because I want you to suffer.) You need to make sure you're not spending more money than you make. If you don't, then you may end up in debt, being hunted down by random collection agencies and selling your favorite Fendi bag on eBay to make ends meet. So make sure you're in the clear by subtracting your total monthly expenses from your monthly income. That equals your total monthly cash flow—aka how much money you have left over.

My Total Monthly Cash Flow

$3,000 my monthly income
– $1,500 my total monthly expenses
_____
$1,500 my total monthly cash flow

Ideally, your total monthly cash flow should in the positive instead of the negative. If it's not, it's time to rethink your finances.

First option: Cut the expenses you don't need. If you and your boyfriend live off cell phones, don't waste your money on a landline. If you have a gym membership and haven't even broken a sweat in the past two months, it's time to call it quits. If you spend a couple hundred dollars a month getting your hair dyed, then maybe it's time to go natural. (Come on, brunettes can have more fun, too.)

Second option: Get a cheaper apartment. If the apartment you want will bleed you dry, don't get it. Find a place that won't drive you into debt. If that's not a good alternative, consider option three: Rethink how you want to split your shared expenses. If your boyfriend is making Warren Buffet money and you only make bartender money, you may want to reconsider the fifty-fifty split. Instead, think about splitting your shared expenses by percentage.

Kenneth, from Cincinnati, came up with a similar solution when his girlfriend moved in with him. At the time, he was making four times as much money as she was. Not only that, but she was moving into his house, which had a high monthly mortgage. If he'd split everything fifty-fifty with her, she would've been broke in about...oh...two months' time. Kenneth obviously didn't want that to happen, so he worked out a seventy-five–twenty-five split that allowed his girlfriend to contribute to the mortgage without wiping out her life savings.

So what's a good equation for you? How do you figure it out by percentage? Well, a little formula can help you out. (Yes, another equation.) It's based *purely* on how much money you make per month compared to how much your boyfriend makes. If you make a certain percentage more than him, that's how much more you should be paying in shared monthly expenses (and vice versa). First you need to figure out the total

amount of money you and your boyfriend make per month.
It should look something like this:

Our Combined Monthly Income

    $3,000   my monthly income
+ $5,000   his monthly income
_____

    $8,000   our combined monthly income

Next, take *your* monthly income and divide it by your *combined* monthly income. That will equal the *percentage* of the shared monthly expenses you should be paying. Sound confusing? It may be a little at first, but just stick with it. Here's the sample equation to help you out:

What Percentage of Our Shared Monthly Expenses Should I Be Paying?

    $3,000   my monthly income
÷ $8,000   our combined income
_____

=   0.375   which translates to 37.5 percent, is the
            percentage of the shared monthly
            expenses I have to pay

Phew, this feels like a lot of math for a relationship book, but hang in there. You're almost done. You've figured out the *percentage* of shared monthly expenses you have to pay. All you have to do is multiply that number by your shared monthly expenses, and the total equals how much you have to pay per month. It should look like this:

How Much of Our Shared Total Monthly Expenses I Have to Pay

0.375	percentage of shared monthly expenses *I* have to pay
× $2,000	our shared monthly expenses (rent, TV bill, etc.)
= $750	how much I have to pay per month

That's it. You're finished. That's how much money you have to pay out of the shared monthly expenses. So if you're paying $750 of the shared monthly expenses of $2,000, your boyfriend has to pay the remaining $1,250. Keep in mind that this figure is purely based on your income. Even if your boyfriend is making five times more than you, he may be five times more in *debt* than you. If you want to take this factor into account, subtract your personal expenses from your income before you start this equation.

$3,000 ÷ $8,000
= 0.375

$E=MC^2$

Is this going to be on the test?

Argument #2
"Umm...yeah, that equation is kind of...ridiculous. Not everything is based on simple math."

That's absolutely true, which is why this is only an *example* of how to split your combined expenses. If you don't like the equation, don't use it. Figure out a solution that works for you. Maybe you want to split the rent fifty-fifty and let your boyfriend pay for the TV bill. Or maybe your boyfriend is super successful, and he's offered to pay the rent in exchange for sexual favors. Okay, that last one is a joke. I'm just making sure you're still paying attention. But it still illustrates that you can be creative when splitting your shared expenses. Whatever you do, just figure out a split you can both agree on.

◎ Some Things You Shouldn't Share

In any live-in relationship you'll end up sharing a lot of things with your boyfriend: a bathroom, chores, his electric razor (although he may not be aware of this). But there are some things that you shouldn't share.

Shouldn't Share Item #1: Credit Cards

Here's the thing—your boyfriend doesn't pay for your credit card. You do. You've spent years paying it off in a timely fashion. Sure, you may have racked up a few thousand dollars on mindless purchases (such as jewelry and front-row seats to the Blue Man Group), but you still managed to pay it off. That's why you have such a great credit score. So why risk it all by adding someone else's name to your credit card?

> Argument #1
> "He's not just someone, he's my boyfriend. If I can trust him to see me without makeup (and not run screaming from the room), then I think I can trust him with my MasterCard."

Of course you can trust him. After all, he is the man you're supposed to marry in some elaborate ceremony on the island of Crete. But he's still a human being, which means he could forget to pay a bill. Or forget to tell you about his $500 purchase at Best Buy. And guess what? Now that impulse buy or forgotten payment is permanently on your credit. So don't put yourself in that situation. Keep your credit cards separate.

Shouldn't Share Item #2: Bank Accounts

A lot of new live-in relationshippers think of pooling their money together. Two incomes are better than one, right? Absolutely. But until you say "I do," you should not have a shared bank account, because no legal agreement binds you together. Besides that, you want to make sure your hard-earned cash isn't being spent on items you didn't agree on.

> **Argument #2**
> "My boyfriend isn't a crook. He's not going to rip me off. We'll just set rules about what our shared bank account will be used for."

Alissa, from Philadelphia, had the same philosophy when she moved in with her boyfriend. They had a lot of shared expenses, so they figured a shared bank account would make things easier. They both agreed this account would only be used to pay for their rent and their bills. Then one day Alissa got their bank statement, and she discovered her boyfriend had been using their shared money to buy himself comic books—first-edition, illustrator-signed comic books that totaled $1,000. Apparently, he'd run out of cash of his own, so he had dipped into their joint account to pay for his little hobby.

So what did Alissa do? Lots of screaming, yelling, and swearing that would make a truck driver blush. Her boyfriend got the message, sold the comics, and promised he'd never do it again. But Alissa wasn't sure whether she could trust him. What if he took up some other random hobby—such as curling—and wanted to use their shared bank funds to feed his needs? Alissa didn't want to risk it, so she closed their account. It was the best solution for their relationship.

Shouldn't Share Item #3: Co-signer Responsibilities
Avoid cosigning the loan for your boyfriend's new car (or motorcycle, or Segway, or whatever his vehicle of choice is). Yes, you may feel the urge to give in to his puppy-dog eyes when he asks for your help, but don't do it. If his credit isn't good enough to get a car on his own, there's a reason for that. So don't let yourself get talked into a cosigner role. Because if the two of you ever break up, you'll be forever tied to him and his 1987 Chevy Impala—and so will your credit.

By now you've read through this section (begrudgingly) and have a firm grasp on what to do regarding joint credit cards, joint bank accounts, or joint whatever. But just to be sure, take this quiz to see how far you've truly come.

✳ **QUIZ: Some Things You Shouldn't Share** ✳

Your boyfriend has his eye on a new laptop. He's been researching it for months and knows this is just the one for him. One problem—he doesn't have enough money to buy it. He comes to you and asks if he could put it on your credit card and promises he'll pay it back on a month-to-month basis. You:

(cont'd.)

QUIZ (cont'd.)

1. hand over your credit card and say, "Sounds great. And buy yourself a new outfit while you're at it."

2. think it over and ask, "What's your month-to-month plan?"

3. say, "That computer looks fantastic. You should definitely get it. Why don't you ask your mom, dad, sister, brother, or best friend for the money? Better yet, why don't you apply for a credit card? That way you can pay for it yourself."

The correct answer is option 3. Don't let yourself fall into a bad situation. Remember, loving your boyfriend does not make you responsible for him. If he truly needs someone to cosign for something, then he should ask one of his family members for help, not you.

Chapter Checklist

Remember the following when dealing with money matters:

☐ Discuss your finances (how much you make and how much you owe). Don't be embarrassed if you're in debt up to your eyeballs. Your boyfriend will love you anyway.

☐ Decide how to split your shared expenses. Remember, not everything has to be fifty-fifty (especially if he's making CEO money and you're making IOU money).

☐ If your boyfriend thinks it's a good idea to have a shared credit card or bank account, *don't agree to it*. If you can barely handle sharing a toothbrush, why take on someone else's finances?

5

Your Stuff Belongs in a Garage Sale

*G*ood news: You've picked out the perfect place to live, decided on your move date, had all the awkward conversations, and now it's finally here—moving time. But suddenly you notice something. You have a lot of stuff...and your boyfriend has a lot of stuff. So how exactly is all this stuff supposed to fit into one tiny apartment?

Bad news: It's not all going to fit. You may have to trash your papasan chair, and your boyfriend may have to dump his broken-in recliner. But don't stress over it too much, because this chapter will help you figure out what to keep, what to toss, and where to put everything once you've made the big move.

Give this lamp the boot.

◎ Packrats

Let's be honest: Moving sucks. You have to box things up, throw things out, and streamline your entire life. But you must remember one key point: You're merging your life with your boyfriend's, so you've got to make room for him. First step: Open up your closet and figure out what you actually need.

> **Argument #1**
> "For your information, I need everything that's in there. Why else would I have kept it all for so long?"

Maybe it's because you're a packrat. Sure, nobody ever wants to believe this. Maybe your friend is a pack-rat, or your aunt, or that crazy cat lady from *Hoarders*. But definitely not you. And you know, you could be right. You may not be one of those anal-retentive, can't-throw-things-away packrats, but you could share a few of the same qualities.

Here's how to figure it out. Take a look around your apartment. Are you holding on to old papers from your seventh-grade English class? Do you keep old, broken furniture just so you can drape your clothes over it? Do you still own a pair of *Alf* pajamas that you haven't fit into since the late '80s?

If you answered "yes" to any of these questions, then you may be a packrat. In other words, you're a member of the "just-in-case" sorority. You hold on to an item "just in case" you may need it. You keep purses that are out of date "just in case" they come back in style. You hold on to that scrunchie from middle school "just in case" you want to wear a high ponytail. You tuck away that *New Kids on the Block* T-shirt "just in case" the band becomes relevant again.

I used to be a member of the "just in case" sorority, too. I would hold on to countless items "just in case" a situation would arise where I'd need my gold parachute pants. But everything changed when my boyfriend moved in. He spent hours trying to fit all his clothes into the one inch of closet space I'd given him. When he couldn't manage, he politely asked me to get rid of the things I didn't need so he would have room. I, of course, refused. I'd already gotten rid of everything I didn't need. And that's when he said, "Really? You need this *Sleepless in Seattle* VHS case, even though you don't have the tape *or* a VCR?"

That comment hit home. Not just because I missed seeing Tom Hanks and Meg Ryan's undeniable chemistry, but because my boyfriend was right—I didn't need the VHS case. Just like I didn't need my broken duck-shaped phone or the collection of flannel shirts from my grunge phase. But I was holding onto it all for a ridiculous reason—just in case.

Live-In ☀ Lesson

Stop thinking about "just in case" and start thinking in the present. If you don't need it now, you probably don't need it at all.

So dive into your closet and decide what to keep and what to chuck. And be honest with yourself. If you haven't worn that skirt in the past year, you'll probably never wear it again. Toss it. If you have shoes that don't fit anymore, throw them out. If that's too painful, then donate them to Goodwill, to a shelter, or to a best friend in need. Just get rid of them.

If you're still not sure what to keep and what to toss, then use the following as a guideline.

Trash an Item If...

- it's part of a pair and you can't find its match.

- it scares your cat and it's not supposed to.

- it's always falling apart and you've glued it back together more than once.

- your friends point and laugh at it, asking if you stole it from a traveling circus.

- it doesn't work, and it never has.

Those are a few ideas to get you started. Now open up your closet, dig through your stuff, and get rid of all the "just in cases." You're combining your life with your boyfriend's, so the least you can do is give him enough closet space to survive.

◎ Furniture Wars

You've trashed the stuff you don't need, but you're still left with a dilemma. You and your boyfriend have duplicates of some items (such as couches, chairs, and painfully out-of-date coffeemakers). So now what are you supposed to do? He loves his stuff just as much as you love yours, but there's no way two couches will fit in one apartment. Yes, you can measure the space just to be sure, but you know it's pointless. So how do you decide whose stuff to keep and whose to toss?

*Number One: Consider the condition
of each piece of furniture.*
If your boyfriend's couch is some torn, lumpy mess that sinks when you sit in it and your couch is as soft as a marshmallow, the decision is pretty easy: Choose the one that's in better condition. This may be hard for him (or you) to deal with, but you have to think about what's best for the two of you and what's best for your apartment.

Number Two: Consider the sentimental value.

You probably each have your own set of silverware, mugs, sake glasses, and so forth, but your kitchen only includes so much cabinet space. You may have an elegant dish set from Williams-Sonoma, but your boyfriend may not want to use it. Why? Because those dishes don't mean anything to him, but the *Star Wars* collectible glasses he's had for more than fifteen years do. So don't discount your boyfriend's worn-down cups, because when it comes to nostalgia, you do have to give a little. Besides, even you've got to admit that Boba Fett tumbler looks pretty cool.

What if you weigh the sentimental value against the condition of the piece of furniture and you still can't decide what to do? That's when you bargain. And bargaining is much better than battling any day. So stop with the name calling and the evil looks—instead, make a trade. If he desperately wants to keep his beer can–shaped table, let him—just as long as you get to keep your vintage ruby-red loveseat (or whatever else you're trying to hold on to).

So look at the identical items that you and your boyfriend have and start compromising. If compromising doesn't get you anywhere, then make a game of it. Poker, Yahtzee, Monopoly—choose your poison. Just remember, the winner takes all.

> Argument #2
> "We're talking about my brand-new bamboo dresser. You want me to play rock, paper, scissors to figure out whether it should stay or go? No way."

Moving in together is already a high-pressure situation. So don't let some itsy-bitsy piece of furniture sour your relationship. In the grand scheme of things, it's really not that important. Think about it. If you had to choose between your Ikea Poäng chair and your boyfriend, which one would you choose? Yes, that's a silly question, but people tend to get a little silly when it comes to their stuff.

If you ever feel yourself starting a furniture war, just remember that your boyfriend's feelings are way more important than your personal possessions. So let it go—unless that piece of furniture is a massage chair. That's definitely worth fighting for.

🌀 Decorating for Two

For many of us, designing is fun. It gives you a chance to flex your styling muscles and spend money on things you ordinarily wouldn't buy (such as fancy lamps and coffee tables in the shapes of iconic celebrities). But before you get ahead of yourself, make sure you include your boyfriend on any design decisions that come your way. Sure, he probably doesn't even know how to color coordinate his own sock drawer, but that doesn't matter. You're decorating his apartment, too, so make sure the look reflects both of your tastes.

> **Argument #1**
> "But why? My taste is so much better than his, so why should I risk a potential designing disaster?"

Thea, from San Francisco, felt the same way when she moved in with her boyfriend. She knew that, except for his taste in women, he had the worst taste on the planet. So she did what she thought any good girlfriend would do: She waited until he fell asleep and arranged the apartment in the perfect feng shui pattern. She figured she was doing her boyfriend a favor, but he...didn't exactly see it that way. In fact, he said he felt like a prisoner in his own home.

That wasn't the reaction Thea had been looking for. She had expected him to be elated and to throw fresh roses at her feet out of gratitude. Instead, he was pissed off, which pissed her off. She had slaved for hours organizing their place perfectly, and all he could do was complain about it. Thea's boyfriend didn't take the bait. He told her what the real problem was—she had designed the apartment without him. She had kept him out of their first big decision together.

The same problem can arise from impromptu designing decisions. Admit it. You've probably been out somewhere, minding your own business, when bam—you spot the lime-green side table of your dreams. Instinctively, you may reach for your no-limit credit card, but resist the urge. Instead, call your boyfriend, because you should never buy furniture for your apartment without talking it over with him first.

> Argument #2
> "Why? I'm the one who's paying for it."

You can't just go around buying whatever your heart desires, because it's not just your apartment. Your boyfriend lives there, too. And guess what? He may not like your taste in furniture. (Shocking, but it's possible.) So talk to him about it prepurchase. Find out if he even wants that new lime-green side table, or zebra-skin love-seat, or whatever it is you want to buy. The last thing you want is to show up with something shiny and new and have your boy-friend say, "No, we're not keeping that piece of dreckitude."

Live-In ☀ Lesson

It doesn't matter how great your taste is. You're sharing your apartment with your boyfriend, so his opinion counts, too.

Do not let your inner diva take over the designing process. Ask your boyfriend's opinion about everything. Let him set up some things (with your consultation, of course). Invite him to join you on your furniture-buying adventures. If you don't, then your little designing obsession may have a negative affect on your relationship. How do you know if you've reached this level? Well, if you hear your boyfriend say any of the following statements, then you may just be a designing diva.

- ❀ This place is like a museum. Am I even allowed to touch anything?

- ❀ When did you start channeling Martha Stewart?

- ❀ I love what you've done with the place. Now where do I live?

- ◉ It doesn't feel like there's any space here for me.

- ◉ At least at my own place, I didn't feel like a caged animal.

That's really not the type of thing you want to hear from your boyfriend. If he's said anything like this to you, then it's time to apologize. That's right, own up to being a diva and then immediately ask for your boyfriend's help in the designing process. And try to act like you actually mean it.

Let's just pretend that you are a super-duper girlfriend who decides to hear your boyfriend out when it comes to decorating. What if his ideas are terrible? What if he wants to decorate the apartment with hideous stuff, such as antique bottle caps or boars' heads? Unfortunately, this is more common than you think. A lot of boyfriends out there come armed with ugly furniture, bizarre keepsakes, and other items that (their girlfriends think) should be thrown into a bottomless pit.

So how in the world are you supposed to mesh his raggedy stuff with your fantastic stuff? It's a little thing called give and take. The same thing you did with splitting your furniture is what you'll have to do here—compromise.

When my boyfriend moved in with me, he brought along his Aztec spear, his Geronimo painting, his skull masks, and his sculpture of two cats making love (and those were the most normal items). Did he want to put everything up? Of course. Did I let him? Absolutely not, because I wasn't comfortable having a tribal mask directly above our bed. That didn't work for me. But I did allow him to hang his spear over our closet door. That was my compromise.

It's your turn. Take a look through your boyfriend's stuff. If you're at all frightened by what you see, just take a break and check back when you've recovered. Now pick out a few items of his that you actually like (yes, you do have to choose something) and have your boyfriend do the same with your stuff. Once you have

This spear goes perfectly with the rug.

those approved items, start placing them around your apartment. This way you're decorating together *and* using stuff from both of you in the process.

Chapter Checklist

Don't fight over furniture. Review these tips instead:

☐ Stop being a packrat. If you haven't seen it, worn it, or thought about it in the past year, get rid of it.

☐ When it comes to identical furniture items, decide whose to keep and whose to dump. Consider each item's condition, sentimental value, and whether it would be embarrassing to have around the house.

☐ No one likes a diva (unless it's Whitney Houston or Mariah Carey). So take a deep breath and smile when your boyfriend displays his miniature macaroni Leaning Tower of Pisa. No one said compromise was easy.

☐ Never buy furniture for your apartment without discussing it with your boyfriend first. After all, not everyone is a fan of leopard-print upholstery.

6

But Your Cat Bites

*P*eople love their pets. Some people dress their pets up in fancy little outfits and call them names like Fluffers or Lord Anthony. Other people refer to their pets as "children" or their "only friends." Some people even spend hundreds of dollars on pet therapy, pet massages, and fashionable pet hairdos just to make sure their pets are as happy as humanly possible (or at least as petly possible).

But what if you aren't one of those people? What if you're a pet-free person who suddenly has pet ownership thrust upon her? That's mainly who this chapter is for—the girlfriend getting ready to be a new "mother" to her boyfriend's beloved furry child. This chapter will help you deal with the challenges you'll face—even when you feel frustrated enough to "cut the leash" on your adopted pet forever.

◎ Taking Care of Business

Congratulations—you're not just moving in with your boyfriend. You're moving in with your boyfriend's little kitty, doggy, tarantula, or other random foreign species. That's

This was not part of the deal.

right. A new bundle of joy is coming into your life, so you need to prepare for it. How do you do this? By having a conversation with your boyfriend. (Uh-huh, another conversation.) You need to clarify who's going to be responsible for this pet. Will it be him, you, Siegfried and Roy? Sure, you probably assume that your boyfriend's going to handle everything (because it's his pet), but he may have a different idea. So sit down, talk it out, and figure out how this little furball will affect your live-in situation.

Step #1: Write out a list of pet chores.

If you've had a pet before, then you already know what to expect. If you haven't, be prepared for the shock of your life. People sometimes refer to their pets as children, because they take just as much work. You have to walk it (if it's a dog), clean out the litter box (if it's a cat or a highly trained Chihuahua), feed it, play with it, brush its hair, and sometimes even sing it to sleep.

Okay, that last one is an exaggeration, but you can see that pet ownership includes a lot of responsibilities, so make note of them all. Depending on what type of animal you have (gerbil, lizard, or orangutan), your list may be a bit longer or shorter. Either way, come up with your own personal list of pet chores. You'll need it for the next step.

Step #2: Decide who's doing what.

Does your boyfriend expect you to help him with the pet chores? Do you even want to? Technically, this is his pet, so you really have no responsibility. But any good girlfriend knows that it doesn't hurt to give a little. Besides, your boyfriend's pet is going to be your new roommate. So if you want to stay on Fido's good side, it's best to pitch in with the pet chores.

> **Argument**
> "This is a pet, not a human being. I'm sorry, but if I don't clean up after my boyfriend, then why should I clean up after his pet?"

The difference is that your boyfriend is capable of cleaning up after himself (at least in theory). His pet...not so much (unless it has somehow developed opposable thumbs and knows how to work a pooper scooper). So if the cat's litter box starts to smell, don't expect Frisky to run in there and clean it out. The cat doesn't know how to, but you do.

Step #3: Talk costs.

When your boyfriend takes his German shepherd in for a yearly checkup, does he assume that you'll be splitting the bill? If his Siamese cat runs out of wet food, does he expect you to stop by the pet store to pick up another can? What about your boyfriend's very old (and very ill) pet ferret? Are you supposed to pitch in and help pay for its monthly medication? These are all things you and your boyfriend need to discuss up front. Technically, the ball is in your court. This is your boyfriend's pet—not yours—so you're under no obligation to pay for things. Just make sure to fill your boyfriend in ahead of time, because he may have different expectations.

But what if you're different? What if you've accepted your boyfriend's pet skunk into your life and are more than willing to split the costs? Before you break out your checkbook, first make sure you can afford it. Sure, you may be okay with the idea of paying the vet bills, but is that expense actually in your budget? Flip back to Chapter 4 to determine whether you have enough extra income to put into the pot. Why? Because pets are a lot more expensive than you think.

Typical Pet Expenses

- ⊛ food
- ⊛ clothes (optional, of course, but who doesn't want to dress up a rabbit in a ballerina outfit?)

- vet bills (basic checkups, surgery, teeth cleanings, vaccinations, medications, overnight stays, and so forth)

- toys (seriously, Lassie likes a lot of variety, so be prepared to pay for a wide assortment of chew toys)

- hygiene (nail clippers, toothbrush, hairbrush, flea baths, and doggie breath mints)—trust me, nothing's worse than a bulldog with morning breath.

Those are just a handful of pet expenses. It may not look like a lot, but it adds up over time. So figure out what you can afford. If you can only manage a bag of kitty litter, don't sweat it. That's better than nothing. Don't feel obligated to put in more than your budget can handle (or more than you want to give). As long as you can accept this pet as part of your new live-in family, your boyfriend will be more than satisfied.

⊚ House Rules

Pets can be sweet, loving, adorable little animals. But, unfortunately, they're not like this all the time. In fact, sometimes they can be downright evil. (Think *Pet Cemetery*. Sure, they were all possessed, but you get the point.) How is that possible? How can

That is not a chew toy!

your boyfriend's cute Labrador turn into one of Satan's creatures? Honestly, it's not a far stretch. Pets are still animals, which means they like to chew, bite, and pee all over things. And inevitably, those "things" will be your property. If you haven't experienced this firsthand, then get ready for a big surprise.

Bad Things Your Boyfriend's Pet May Do to Your Stuff

- ⊛ You know that bedspread you spent days tracking down? Yeah, your boyfriend's cat may just poop on it.

- ⊛ Your favorite four-inch pumps? Be prepared for your boyfriend's doggy to nibble that heel down to two inches. (You really should've bought him a chew toy.)

- ⊛ Did you bring home a project from work? Well, if it's paper, the cat may "mistake" it for the litter box and pee all over it. (That's your cat's way of saying, "Give me more attention—or else.")

- ⊛ Your brand-new leather couch? Guess what? That sweet little puppy may decide to rip it to shreds. (The puppy may not even have a reason for doing so other than just being bored.)

This list isn't supposed to scare you—it's supposed to prepare you for what may happen. If and when your boyfriend's pet acts out, you want to have a plan of action.

What's the best way to discipline his pet? A little tap on the butt, a spray with the water bottle, or no treats for the day? It's really up to you and your boyfriend. Just make sure you both agree on a solution. If you don't, the pet may keep on acting out. And if that happens, there's a good chance it'll put a strain on your relationship.

> **Argument**
> "Now that's just silly. Pets can't cause that much trouble."

Jane thought the same thing when she moved in with her boyfriend and his miniature schnauzer, Monty. But her opinion quickly changed when she found his dog taking a bite out of her Guess bag. Was she pissed off? Absolutely, but she didn't discipline him, because he wasn't her dog. Instead, she told her boyfriend about it. He simply laughed and said, "Oh, Monty was just playing." So Jane shrugged it off, until she found Monty digging his claws into her Prada purse. When she pointed it out, her boyfriend responded with, "Dogs do that."

At that point, Jane was furious—not just at Monty but at her boyfriend, too. She felt like he was putting his dog's feelings before her own. So the next time little Monty tore into her designer duds, she yelled at him. Did that help the situation? Well, yes and no. Yes, because Monty stopped treating her stuff like doggie treats. And no, because her boyfriend got upset that she disciplined his dog without consulting him first.

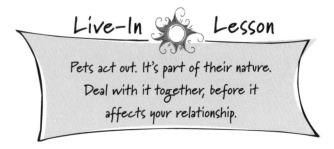

Live-In 🌞 Lesson

Pets act out. It's part of their nature. Deal with it together, before it affects your relationship.

Another thing you need to discuss—pets in the bedroom. What are the ground rules? Should you let your pet sleep in bed with you? That's a tough dilemma. For some, it's a matter of hygiene. If your boyfriend's Persian cat has been digging up dirt in the backyard, then you probably don't want her trailing mud onto your satin sheets. If your boyfriend's cocker spaniel is a bit of a drooler, then you should probably keep him away from your pillow.

But what if your boyfriend doesn't mind those things? What if he's okay with his pet iguana leaving dirty paw tracks all over the bedspread? Or he can handle sleeping with his poodle's irritable bowel syndrome? If this sounds a little cringe-worthy to you, then you two need to discuss his pet's sleeping arrangements before it becomes an issue. Yes, your boyfriend may have slept with his cat Snowflake for ten years, but that doesn't mean you have to.

So what's the solution? Compromise. Maybe you don't want your boyfriend's dog sleeping on your pillow, but you will allow him to sleep at the end of the bed. If you've got a slight cat allergy, then don't let his calico sleep with her tail in your face. Let her enjoy the comfort of the bedroom floor. Just come up with solutions that work best for both of you. If your boyfriend refuses to go along with that, stand your ground. Because if he has to choose between sleeping with you or his pet, he'll pick the one that doesn't have fleas. Hopefully that's you.

◎ Allergy Solutions

Allergies. Yep, with live-in pets your allergies don't just come once a year, they show up on a daily basis. So what can you do about it? Before you donate your boyfriend's pup to some celebutante's handbag, take some time to explore ways to reduce your allergies first.

The easiest option (other than breaking out the electric shaver)? Over-the-counter pills or nose sprays. That's right, you can buy your allergy relief in a bottle from your local drugstore. For some, this may solve the problem. You take an allergy pill whenever you're feeling a little stuffed up and *voilà*—your allergies are relieved for a good twelve hours. But if that doesn't work, you may have to move on to the next level.

Air purifiers are little fanlike machines that help reduce the allergens (such as dust, pollen, pet dander, etc.) in the air that cause allergy attacks. Most likely it'll take a few weeks with a purifier before you'll notice a difference, but it's definitely a good (and affordable) investment. And you can find them just about anywhere—online, in stores, in catalogs, etc. Just make sure to do your research first so you find the one that best fits your needs.

How else can you fight pet allergies? You can de-dander your boyfriend's pet, because it's not the pet hair you're allergic to, it's the pet dander. If you can reduce the amount of dander the pet produces, you can cut down your allergy attacks. Most de-dandering products can be found at your local pet store in the form of dander-reducing shampoos, wipes, and sprays. Combine that with frequent pet hair brushing and trimming, and you should be good to go.

What if none of those solutions works for you? Then it's time to check with your doctor. Most likely your physician will recommend allergy shots on a continuous basis. Yes, this option may sound painful, but at least it would help reduce your allergies over time. In some cases, it could clear them up altogether. This may seem like an extreme course of action for an animal, but it's worth it (at least, for your boyfriend's sake).

If none of these solutions solves your allergy problem, find one that does, because you don't want to be the reason your boyfriend gets rid of his pet. That would be like his asking you to get rid of your personal trainer or chop off your pinkie, so avoid this situation as much as you can.

For some of you, this may not be possible. Maybe your allergies are so bad that you can't be within a hundred feet of an animal without breaking out in hives. And although you love your man (and his pet), you don't want to look like Swamp Thing for the rest of your life.

If that's the case, then it's time to find a new home for your boyfriend's cuddly little friend. Sure, this will be hard on him, but he knows that your health is more important. So work together to place Whiskers with a close friend, coworker, family member, or loving pet owner. That way he'll still have an opportunity to visit his pet—or at least know that it's in a happy home with an endless supply of toys and treats.

◎ Buying New Pets

You two are moving in together, so what better way to break in your new place than by getting a new pet? Bad idea. That's kind of like getting your first perm on prom night. Why? Because first, you need to see if your live-in situation works *before* you bring anything else into the equation.

> **Argument**
> "It's a pet, not a baby. So if our relationship doesn't work out, it's no biggie."

Actually, it *is* a biggie. If your live-in relationship doesn't work out, you're going to have to figure out what to do with your brand-new pet. Sure, some of you heartless few could drive to the woods and let Rover run free, but what if you got attached to it? What if your boyfriend got attached to it? In the breakup custody battle, who would get to keep the pet?

Layla, a former live-in relationshipper, had to deal with that dilemma herself. When she moved in with her boyfriend, they both thought they were missing something…a cute little puppy. So they bought themselves an adorable miniature schnauzer and named it Hanson. And sure enough, Hanson did make their place a lot homier. But after a few months of living together, they realized that they loved the

puppy much more than they loved their relationship. So they broke up. But what to
do with Hanson?

Layla spent weeks fighting with her
boyfriend, trying to get him to see why
she deserved the puppy more than he
did. She was the one who found him
at the pet store. Then again, her boyfriend was the one who paid for him. So
they decided to share custody. Every two months Layla would
get Hanson, and then her boyfriend would get him for the
next two months. It was a tough decision, but it was the best
arrangement they could come up with.

Live-In ☀ Lesson

Make sure your live-in relationship works
before you go out and get the pet
of your dreams.

Are you ready to say "no" when you see a cute little animal
flashing you their "adopt-me" eyes? Take the pet love quiz to
find out.

✳ ✳ ✳ **QUIZ: Pet Love** ✳ ✳ ✳

One Sunday afternoon, you and your boyfriend decide to take a little walk together. You pass a pet store, go inside, and see an adorable little kitten just purring its eyes out. You love this kitten. Your boyfriend loves this kitten. This kitten loves you right back. And even though you've only lived together for one month, you decide to:

1. buy it right then and there. This kitty is too cute to let go. You have to adopt it.

2. wait a few months. But after just twelve days, you can't resist. You get the kitten. It'll be okay. Your relationship seems to be fine, so this couldn't hurt, right?

3. play with the kitten for a while and then walk away. Yes, you desperately want a pet, but it's better to wait it out.

If you picked option 3, then you aced this quiz. If you didn't, then you may want to go back and reread this section until you get it right.

✳ ✳ ✳ ✳ ✳ ✳ ✳ ✳ ✳ ✳

Chapter Checklist

Here's a quick refresher for dealing with pet problems:

☐ Weekly manicures for your boyfriend's pet don't come cheap. So decide whether you're willing to contribute to those basic (or sometimes unnecessary) pet costs.

☐ Don't let Snuggles get away with pooping in your favorite handbag. Figure out a type of punishment that you and your boyfriend can both agree on.

☐ Consider basic solutions, such as allergy pills, air purifiers, and dander-reducing pet wipes, to help handle your allergy problems.

☐ Don't buy a new pet until your live-in relationship has stabilized. (Well, maybe a fish is okay, but only if it has a really nice color scheme.)

7

Mary Poppins Is on Sick Leave

o you remember the movie *Mary Poppins*? It's a wonderful story about a magical nanny who is the ultimate multitasker. She can dance, she can sing, she can put children to sleep with a spoonful of sugar. Yes, she can do it all. But you should know one important thing about Mary Poppins—she's not real. That's right, you can't hire her to do your domestic duties. Instead, you and your boyfriend will have to figure it out on your own.

When it comes to cooking, cleaning, and all the other chores around the house, prepare yourself—two people living together means twice as much dust, twice as much dirt, and twice as much trail mix in the couch cushions. But before you freak out and call the cleaning police, take a look through this chapter. It'll walk you through how to split chores fairly and teach you how to deal with those little domestic disputes.

◎ Wheel of Chores

No one likes to do chores. They can be gross, time-consuming, and more boring than a PBS special. But, unfortunately, unless you're rich or have a maid on speed dial, you and your boyfriend will be handling the chores yourselves. So take a long look around your apartment and compile a list of all the chores you have to do on a weekly basis (sweeping, vacuuming, and dusting off your boyfriend's "Best Apple Fritters" trophy from 4-H club). Once your list is complete, you and your boyfriend can start figuring out who does what.

Wheel of chores

Argument #1
"We're talking about chores, not brain surgery. It'll work itself out on its own."

Actually, it won't. Because here's a little secret you may not know about guys—most of them don't like to clean. Shocking, right? But it's true. Some guys out there *hate* touching the vacuum, the broom, or the lemon-scented furniture polish. A few even claim to be allergic to laundry detergent. So if you don't talk about the cleaning responsibilities now, your boyfriend may assume he doesn't have any. Save yourself the headache and make it known that you'll *both* be doing chores, and then figure out how to split them.

The most common solution is the fifty-fifty split: You take numbers one through five on the chore list, and your boyfriend takes six through ten. Each week swap chores so you won't get stuck doing the one you hate on a continuous basis. Another option is to split chores according to what you like/dislike/vaguely tolerate. Maybe your boyfriend has grown strangely attached to the floor sweeper. If that's the case, let him handle sweeping while you take on something you prefer. Either way, just make sure you're both happy with the split.

While you're at it, discuss any cleaning pet peeves. Do you lose it when you see a streak on your freshly washed window? Do you cry if the bathroom tile isn't scrubbed with a toothbrush? Do you have an emotional breakdown if you find dust bunnies under the futon? If so, you may want to talk to your boyfriend (or a therapist) about these kinds of issues before they turn into a potential domestic dispute.

> Argument #2
> "You want me to discuss my pet peeves, too? Forget it. There's no reason for my boyfriend to think I'm any more anal than I already am."

Anne, a live-in relationshipper, felt the same way when she moved in with her boyfriend. She didn't want to bother him with her huge pet peeve—crumbs. Yep, she hated seeing crumbs on the floor, on the couch, on her five hundred–thread-count sheets. But she decided not to tell her boyfriend, because she didn't want to freak him out.

The problem was that Anne discovered that her boyfriend was a huge crumb-dropper—bread crumbs, cookie crumbs, cracker crumbs, you name it. Anne tried to overlook it until the day she found a lone cheese cracker resting on the carpet. That's when she snapped. She started screaming at her boyfriend about his "crumb problem" and demanded that he get it under control. Her boyfriend was shocked. He had no idea this had been bothering her for so long, because she had never talked to him about it.

Live-In 🌟 Lesson

Talk about your pet peeves up front so you and your boyfriend can deal with them together.

So discuss chores ahead of time. Yes, it'll be a boring conversation, but it's worth it. Because the more you know about each other's likes and dislikes around the house, the less time you'll spend fighting about them later.

🌀 Don't Call Me a Nag

Nobody likes a nag, but there's a good chance that at some point in your relationship, you'll become one. How is this possible? How will you make that turn from a sane, laid-back girlfriend to a finger-pointing, nag machine? Well, it'll start with one of your boyfriend's cute little habits. That one you think is *so* adorable. Except one day, that adorable little habit will start to bother you. So you, being ever so polite, will subtly ask him to stop doing it. And he will subtly pretend he can't hear you. So you'll repeat yourself again and again and again until...you officially become a nag.

Take a deep breath—it's okay. The first step to recovery is to admit that you're a nag. The second step is to understand why you're being this way. Most likely it's because your boyfriend does nag-worthy things. He leaves one square of toilet paper on the roll and doesn't replace it. He drops used tissues all over the coffee table. He leaves the toilet seat up at night and you (of course) half-fall into the toilet at 3:00 AM. Yes, those habits are absolutely, undeniably annoying. But that doesn't mean you should nag him about them.

> **Argument #1**
> "I'm not nagging my boyfriend. I'm simply *reminding* him that he's forgotten to do something."

Constant, unwarranted reminders are a form of nagging. So admit the truth and own up to what you've been doing. If you're still in denial, check out the list below. It'll help you determine whether you are a certified nag queen.

You Know You're a Nag When...

⚘ your boyfriend rolls his eyes and says, "Yes, I *know*. You've told me that *three* times."

- ❀ while you're talking to your boyfriend, he looks you straight in the eye, says nothing, and then turns up the volume on the TV.

- ❀ your boyfriend tells you, "Your mother called. Oops, never mind, I'm already talking to her—it's you."

- ❀ your boyfriend says, "Thanks for telling me that *again*. My short-term memory is shot, so I guess you thought I forgot."

If your boyfriend has said or done any of these things, then you definitely fall into the nag-queen category. So what do you do about it? Cut out the nagging cold turkey, because it doesn't work. If anything, it only encourages your boyfriend to keep doing what he's doing. Why? Because you're treating him like a five-year-old. And guess what? Guys don't like being treated like little boys. As the Village People would say, they want to be treated like macho, macho men.

So if you want your boyfriend to pick up the slack around the house, you only have to do one thing: Tell him exactly what you need him to do, and then—this is the most important part—*leave him alone to do it*. If he doesn't get up immediately, that's okay. He will eventually, because you're not nagging him about it. Instead, you're treating him like an adult.

Argument #2
"But I've tried that, and he still doesn't budge."

That's why you have to put a time limit on your request. If you don't, your boyfriend will definitely take his time doing what you asked him to do. So if you want the dishes done by tomorrow (or whenever), let him know that. If you want the bathroom cleaned before guests arrive, give him a deadline. Just make sure it's a realistic one. If you ask your boyfriend to take out the garbage in the middle of the World Series, it won't get done, because Derek Jeter is a lot more important to your boyfriend than a stinky trash bag. So make sure your requests are within reason to prevent any sort of conflict.

What if you tell your boyfriend what you want, set a time limit, and still see no movement on his part? Then it's time for you two to come up with a solution you both can live with. If he refuses to clean out the toilet, then you should take on that responsibility and add an extra chore to his list. If your boyfriend wants to drink from the milk carton (even though you've repeatedly pointed out how gross it is), then don't nag him about it anymore. Let him keep the milk carton and start buying an extra one for yourself. Stop fighting him and come up with a solution that will make you both happy.

I had to do this myself when I first moved in with my boyfriend. He was, to put it politely, a complete and utter slob. He would leave his clothes all over the bedroom, bathroom, kitchen, and even behind the TV. I couldn't stand it, so I constantly nagged him about it. Did it work? Only for a few hours, and then his socks, T-shirts, and Bermuda shorts would mysteriously make their ways back to the places they didn't belong. I tried being direct with him, but that approach didn't work, either. So we had only one thing left to do—compromise.

We decided that he could have one messy area—one specified spot in the apartment where he could let loose and be a complete slob. In return, I couldn't nag him about it. I had to bite my tongue and look the other way. Was this a bizarre compromise? Absolutely, but it worked. His entire mess stayed confined to one room. So he was happy, and I was happy (especially because he stopped referring to me as the nag fairy).

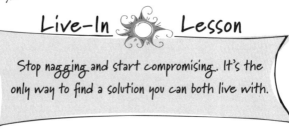

Live-In Lesson

Stop nagging and start compromising. It's the only way to find a solution you can both live with.

◎ Cooking 101

Some people are natural-born cooks, and others are lucky enough to live with them. But what if neither you nor your boyfriend falls into that category? What if you hate the idea of cooking (unless you're watching someone on the Food Network do it)? Then what? How do you work out who cooks when you don't have a chef in the house?

Love is a dish best served over easy.

Once again, embrace the fifty-fifty split. Let your boyfriend cook half the week and you cook the other half. If that plan works for you, then great, wonderful, problem averted. Just make sure to discuss this cooking schedule with your boyfriend before you pick up that whisk.

> **Argument**
> "I'm tired of talking! I'm sure if I cook, my boyfriend will pitch in."

Melissa, from Nashville, thought the same thing. One day she picked up a cookbook and started baking soufflés so fluffy that Julia Child would have turned green with envy. And Melissa just assumed that at some point her boyfriend would join her in the cooking duties. When he didn't, she called him out on it. His response: He never asked her to cook in the first place. So technically, he didn't have to pitch in unless he wanted to.

Ouch. That was not the response Melissa was hoping for. But after a hard-fought argument filled with screaming, crying, and burnt rigatoni, Melissa saw his point. She had never discussed the meal-making duties with her boyfriend—she had just *assumed* that once she started cooking, he'd do the same thing. And her boyfriend had *assumed* that he didn't have to. (And apparently he also assumed that he had his very own live-in chef.)

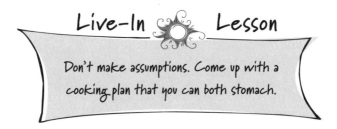

Live-In Lesson

Don't make assumptions. Come up with a cooking plan that you can both stomach.

Discuss the cooking responsibilities. Decide if you want to do a fifty-fifty split, eighty-twenty, or something else. Who knows, maybe you'll agree to do all the cooking if your boyfriend always washes the dishes. Or maybe you'll decide to each make your own meals. Or maybe you'll both give up food altogether and subsist on protein shakes. That's fine, too. Whatever solution you come up with, just make sure to discuss it first so you won't have any food-related surprises.

Chapter Checklist

Prevent domestic disputes by following these guidelines:

☐ Decide how you want to split those icky chores *before* your boyfriend thinks he can skip them for all eternity.

☐ Stop being a nag. Instead, let your boyfriend know what you need him to do and set a time limit. While you're at it, try to compromise.

☐ Don't let cooking duties come between you and your boyfriend. Remember, take-out is just a phone call away.

8

Reality Bites

*Y*ou've done it. You've moved in together. You're enjoying the bliss of sharing space, sharing lives, and sharing endless hours together. You have a thought, and he says it out loud. He starts a sentence, and you finish it for him. It's the perfect live-in relationship, and you couldn't ask for anything more. In fact, you're wondering why you waited so long to move in together in the first place.

But what if you're on the opposite side of the spectrum? Your live-in is not so blissful. It's not so perfect. It's downright annoying. Those endless hours you two spend together are, well, endless. When he says your thought out loud, you roll your eyes. When you finish his sentence, he pretends like he doesn't hear you. It's far from being the ideal situation. In fact, you're starting to wonder why you moved in with your boyfriend in the first place.

Whether you're at the highest of the highs or the lowest of the lows with your live-in relationship, take a few minutes off to explore this chapter. It'll help you deal with your boyfriend during the good times, the bad times, and the in-between times.

🌀 I Didn't Know I Had a Siamese Twin

Do you absolutely positively love spending time with your boyfriend? Have you stopped answering the phone, because you'd rather hear the melodic sound of his voice? Does your boyfriend follow you to the bathroom, because he can't stand being away from your side? Do you hand-feed each other, because you believe it makes the meal taste better?

If this sounds like you, then it's time to call the relationship police. Because the amount of time you've spent with your boyfriend should be a federal offense. That's right—you two have become so obsessed with each other that you've forgotten about everything else. If you're unsure whether you've fallen into this category, then check out the warning signs below.

Signs You've Been Spending Too Much Time with Your Boyfriend

- You've forgotten all your friends' birthdays, graduations, and first names.

- Your boyfriend is growing out his hair to look exactly like yours.

◉ You no longer feel the need to speak to your boyfriend. You're so in tune with one another that you can communicate through smiles, winks, and suggestive eyebrow raises.

◉ The saying "I can't live without you" has become a literal meaning.

◉ People no longer call you two by your given names. Instead, they combine them into things like Bennifer (Ben + Jennifer), Glaren (Glen + Karen), and Fransabelle (Frank + Isabelle).

Be honest, can you relate to any of those things? If so, then it's time to break out of your love cocoon and get back your solo identity. How do you do this? First step: Leave your boyfriend's side and hang out with your friends or family immediately.

If you're starting to panic, that's okay. It's normal. Just breathe into a paper bag, recite a few Buddhist chants, and then come back to this page. Because even though spending time away from your boyfriend seems unnatural, it's absolutely necessary. Here are a few reasons why.

Reason #1: Spending time apart is healthy.
If you've been tied to your boyfriend's hip for the past seventy-two hours, then you're treating him like your personal oxy-

gen tank. You're acting like you can't live (or breathe) without him. And when it comes time to leave each other's side (to go to work or to Bloomingdale's), you'll need to know how to function on your own. You won't know how to do this if you're always dependent upon each other.

Reason #2: You need someone else to vent to.

Sure, it's great that you can tell your man just about anything, but what about the things you can't tell him? Better yet, what about the things he doesn't want to hear? Like stories about that coworker you can't stand. You can only complain so many times about her clipping her toenails at her desk before your boyfriend gets bored. And what about those little nuances you can't stand about your boyfriend? At some point, you're going to want to vent about them. And who are you supposed to turn to then?

Your friends, your family, and your confidantes. If you've been a bad friend or relative since your cohabitation began, then your BFF may not want to hear what you have to say. In fact, she may not even answer your call (or text, or e-mail, or IM message filled with apologetic emoticons). So keep these people close to you, return their calls, and hang out with them from time to time. Because if you don't, you may not have a support system when you need it.

Reason #3: The more time you spend away from your boyfriend, the more you'll appreciate him.

People say distance makes the heart grow fonder, because it's true. The more space you have from each other, the more you'll realize how lucky you both are. This doesn't mean you should plan a six-month safari to Africa by yourself—that's unnecessary and expensive. Instead, take a few hour-long breathers apart, so you have enough time to miss one another. They'll do you and your relationship some good.

🌀 Communication 101

Are you sick of your boyfriend? Do you dread having to talk to him over dinner? Are you constantly encouraging him to work overtime and "accidentally" falling asleep before he gets home? If so, then it's time to open the lines of communication and tell him exactly what's bothering you—namely, him.

Argument #1
"You want me to tell him that he's the reason why I'm so pissed off? I don't think so. I can just let it go."

Can you? Or will that pent-up, little annoyance boil inside you until you explode? If that's the case, then it's time to stop "letting it go." Tell your boyfriend what's bugging you *before* your frustrations get out of hand.

If your boyfriend is smothering you, tell him. If his table manners make you lose your appetite, point it out. If his sloppiness pushes you to drink, let him know. No matter what the problem is, you two need to discuss it, because he may not even realize his habit bothers you.

> ### Argument #2
> "But I told my boyfriend what was bothering me, and he still hasn't done anything about it."

Maybe that's because you were *hinting* at the issue, instead of being direct. Hinting isn't a good thing. It only leads to mixed signals, major disappointments, and ugly gifts. Think about it. Have you ever told your boyfriend *not* to get you a Valentine's Day gift but instead hinted at how romantic surprises are and how much you love fresh-cut roses? So what happened when V-Day rolled around? You got a big box of *nothing*, because you told your boyfriend you didn't want anything (and he actually assumed you meant what you said).

Here's the thing about guys. You know how they don't get shoes, clothes, or Nicholas Sparks movies? Well, they don't get the art of hinting either. They're just not built that way. So when you hint at something, they'll naturally misread the situation. Just take a look at a few examples below.

What Women Say and How Men Interpret It

Girlfriend #1 Says: "You're watching the game again?" (Meaning: Can't you turn it off so we can do anything else?)

Boyfriend #1 Thinks: "It's pretty obvious that I'm watching the game. Why else would all those guys on TV be wearing football jerseys?"

Girlfriend #2 Says: "It's Saturday night, and you want to order pizza again?" (Meaning: It's Saturday. Why can't we check out that hot sushi place where Paris Hilton was arrested?)

Boyfriend #2 Thinks: "What's wrong with pizza? The pizza place a few blocks over has a two-for-one special."

Girlfriend #3 Says: "Are those your dirty dishes in the sink?" (Meaning: Can you get off your butt and put them in the dishwasher already?)

Boyfriend #3 Thinks: "Of course those are my dishes. It's not like some stranger broke in, ate a bowl of oatmeal, and left the dishes in the sink."

Have you ever experienced any of these scenarios? If so, it's probably because you hinted at the problem instead of being straightforward. So save yourself from another misunderstanding and be direct with your boyfriend. Say exactly what you mean (and mean what you say). It may not solve the problem immediately, but at least he'll finally know what's bothering you—assuming he's paying attention.

◎ Are You Ready to Rumble?

Inevitably, you will reach a point in your relationship where you and your boyfriend can't work something out. When that happens, your first instinct may be to put on the boxing gloves and jump into battle mode. But before you do, ask yourself a few questions. Is this a small, silly problem? Can you let it slide? Has your boyfriend tried to compromise? If you can answer "yes" to any of those questions, you may want to call off the fight. On the other hand, if you've brought up an issue repeatedly and your boyfriend has, well, ignored you, let the bell ring. The fight is *on*.

> **Argument**
> "Wait, you're actually encouraging me to fight? Isn't that kind of a bad thing?"

If you're breaking out actual boxing gloves and getting pointers from Mike Tyson, then yes, it's a bad thing. But a little verbal sparring is perfectly healthy. In fact, it's a great way to release all that negative energy that's been festering inside you. So don't be afraid to fight a little—just as long as you fight fair. All you have to do is follow a few simple guidelines.

Rules for Fighting Fair with Your Boyfriend

- No low blows—That means no insulting each other. Negative remarks about his friends, his family, and his regular release of foul gases should not come into play (unless that's what the fight is about).

- Stick to the issue at hand—*don't* bring up something unrelated that happened two weeks, two months, or two years ago.

- Threats are off limits—If things aren't going your way, don't threaten to withhold sex. You're fighting to reach a mutual agreement, not to have everything work

Don't make me call the referee.

out to your best interest. (Besides, we both know you like sex, too. So don't torture yourself.)

⊛ Don't go to bed angry—It's an oldie, but a goodie. Work out the problem the best you can before going to bed. Because sleeping next to your boyfriend after an unresolved blowup is very awkward, and snuggling will definitely be out of the question.

⊛ Don't start a fight when you're angry about something else—If you've had a bad day, are PMSing, or just found out your favorite show got canceled, wait to bring up whatever's bothering you. Your boyfriend shouldn't be an outlet for your mood-fest.

These guidelines should help you deal with your problems without bringing extra baggage into the mix. But what if they don't help? How do you deal with the tension? Take a break from each other and cool down. Try going for a walk, watching something that'll make you laugh, or losing yourself in a dopey magazine (*Us Weekly* can do wonders for your temperament). Just do something that will change your energy and lighten the mood.

After you've let go of those tense feelings, start rethinking the situation. What exactly are you and your boyfriend fighting about? What are you trying to accomplish? Is it realistic? Is it something you *both* can commit to or only you? Keep these answers in your mind so when you do reconnect with your boyfriend, you'll have a jumping-off point.

By the time you two are ready to talk again, you'll be ready with a new set of ideas and new source of energy (and, ideally, your boyfriend will, too). So don't be afraid to take a break from a fight. It doesn't mean you're giving up on the issue. You're just taking a breather from it.

🌀 This Is My Solitary Life

The two of you have talked, fought, and, in the words of Ari Gold from *Entourage*, hugged it out. Now you're mentally exhausted. When this happens, it's important that you follow one key rule: *Find some alone time for yourself.* You've probably heard this before, which is why you're rolling your eyes right now. But you need this free time to reenergize yourself. Don't believe me? Take the quiz below and find out for yourself.

* * * QUIZ: Solitary Quiz * * *

1. The thought of having yet another conversation with your boyfriend makes you:
   a. Feel all warm and fuzzy inside.
   b. Shrug with indifference.
   c. Run out of the room screaming in fear.

(cont'd.)

QUIZ (cont'd.)

2. When did you last have some time for yourself?
   a. A few days ago.
   b. Two hundred hours, thirty-one minutes, and six seconds ago. But who's counting?
   c. Free time? What's that?

3. On the weekend, your calendar is:
   a. Not-at-all to slightly filled. You do have to make time for your boyfriend.
   b. Mostly filled. You need to get a lot of stuff done. Don't judge.
   c. Filled to capacity. In fact, you're thinking about building a robot to pick up the slack.

Now count up how many As, Bs, and Cs you have.

Mainly As: Okay, you're not desperately in need of "me" time, but you should still make time for yourself. How else are you going to stay balanced?

Mainly Bs: Even though you aren't completely tuckered out, you're getting pretty close. So schedule a "me" date as soon as you can. (And no, that doesn't mean giving yourself an extra minute on your morning commute.)

Mainly Cs: Wow. Call the paramedics, because you need a jolt of "me" time ASAP. So look at your calendar right now, because you need an *immediate* break.

Where exactly should you spend this "me" time? That's up to you. If you can only manage to find a little nook in your apartment, that's fine. If you need the stillness of the great outdoors to find inner peace, go ahead and pitch that tent in Yellowstone Park. Just make sure to do it by yourself. If at any time your boyfriend tries to join you, simply remind him that it's called "me" time and not "we" time for a reason.

How do you know when it's time to take this solo break? If you start to feel overwhelmed, overworked, or overboyfriended, that's your inner Bat-Signal telling you to focus on yourself. It doesn't even have to be a long period of time. If all you have is an extra ten minutes, take it. A little time off is better than nothing at all.

Take a break, or this could happen to you.

What's another good way to stay energized that doesn't involve downing a can of Red Bull? Treat yourself once a week. For some of you, this may be easy. But others among you are thinking, "This is a great idea, but (insert excuse after excuse after excuse for why you can't treat yourself)." Those excuses may sound something like this:

- "I would, but my schedule's filled for the week."

- "My sister's flying in this weekend, and you know how much of a train wreck she is. There's no way I can handle her *and* handle myself."

- "I already know that I have to work late every day this week *and* find time for my boyfriend. Sorry, can't do it."

- "I have no time. I have to plan my neighbor's sister's daughter's kindergarten graduation reception. If I were to back out now, people would talk."

- "I just did something for myself three weeks ago."

If this sounds like you, take a hard look in the mirror and ask yourself, "Why do I keep making excuses to avoid treating myself?" Because when you stop treating yourself, you start to forget yourself. So push those so-called priorities aside and focus on priority number one—you.

Argument
"That sounds really nice, but I can't do that. I just don't have the money."

You don't have to do anything extravagant. No one's telling you to drop $200 on a Shiatsu massage or forcing you to buy a dress made of gold. Just do what you can afford. If that means buying a single chocolate truffle, that's okay. Devour it. If you're too broke to spend any money at all, do something that's free, such as going for a walk in the park or to your favorite gallery.

Now here's a little activity. Come up with a list of all the ways you can treat yourself. Use your imagination. Make the treats big and small, and every week start making your way down the list. When you're done, either start a new list or go back through the same one—just as long as you keep treating yourself over and over again.

Chapter Checklist

Review these guidelines to avoid a relationship meltdown:

☐ Don't let yourself turn into a pod person. Take a break from your boyfriend when you need it.

☐ If you have a problem with your relationship, address it directly. Don't hint around the issue. Remember, most boys don't understand subtlety—or high fashion.

☐ If you're going to fight, make sure to follow the list of guidelines mentioned earlier in the chapter. When it comes to relationships, you should only fight fair.

☐ Take a little "me" time whenever you're feeling drained or overwhelmed. If that doesn't work, treat yourself to some chocolate—lots of chocolate.

9

Your Friends Don't Live Here Anymore

*Y*ou love your friends. They're your support group, your therapists, your lockbox of secrets. They make you laugh when you're depressed and help you home after you've done too many tequila shots. Your friends mean everything to you, which is why you wouldn't want to live without them. But now that you've got a spanking-new live-in relationship, you can't just have them drop by whenever they want.

So how often should your friends be allowed over? Better yet, how often should your boyfriend's? This is a topic all live-ins need to discuss right away. Because even though you think your friends are more fun than a Chris Rock special, your boyfriend may not agree with you, which means having your friends (and their lovely person-

128

alities) over on a consistent basis may not be an option. So how do you compromise? Read on to find out.

◎ Friends Who Never Leave

Your boyfriend loves having his buddies over. If he could have it his way, his BFF would take up permanent residence in your guest bedroom. But what if you aren't okay with that? What if you can only handle his friends visiting once a week? Can he accept that? Or will he go into best-bud withdrawal?

If so, you need to come up with a set amount of friend time you both can agree on. Then test it out for a few weeks and see how it goes. If it works out—wonderful! If it doesn't, keep negotiating until you're both happy.

> **Argument**
> "I don't want to come off as a friend dictator. If he wants his friends to come over whenever, that's fine. We don't need to have a set of rules."

Sure, you could just play it by ear, see what happens, and adjust accordingly. But if your boyfriend is a friend-a-holic and you're a happy hermit, this will cause conflict in your relationship. At some point, you'll go into guest overload and take your wrath out on your man. Don't let this happen. Put these guidelines in place now to avoid any future fights.

What if your boyfriend refuses to compromise? What if he still parades his friends around your apartment twenty-four/ seven? How do you handle this situation? Well, it depends on what kinds of friends he has. And *that* depends on what kind of boyfriend he is: a frat-party boyfriend, a gamer boyfriend, a sports-nut boyfriend, a stoner boyfriend, or a film-/music-geek boyfriend. Take the quiz below to find out what category your guy falls into.

❋   ❋   **QUIZ: What Type of Boyfriend Do You Have?**   ❋   ❋

1. Your boyfriend's idol is:
    a. John Belushi
    b. Pacman
    c. Shaq
    d. Cheech and Chong
    e. Quentin Tarantino
2. Your boyfriend's definition of the perfect Saturday is:
    a. getting so wasted he forgets his own name
    b. spending six hours playing video games

(cont'd.)

QUIZ (cont'd.)

    c. watching a football game and a basketball game on a split screen

    d. lighting up with friends and listening to Pink Floyd

    e. watching a double feature by some pretentious filmmaker you've never heard of

3. Last year, your boyfriend asked Santa for:
   a. another year to haze his brothers
   b. a lifetime subscription to Gamefly
   c. tickets to the World Series
   d. Snacks
   e. front-row seats to the Rolling Stones

4. Your boyfriend is most comfortable wearing:
   a. a beer helmet
   b. a PC gaming headset
   c. a Lakers jersey
   d. a tie-dye shirt decorated with a picture of Jerry Garcia
   e. an iPod

5. Your boyfriend could not live without:
   a. a six pack of good beer
   b. the videogame *Call of Duty: Black Ops*
   c. a Yankees hat
   d. his glass bong
   e. his signed *Taxi Driver* poster

Count up how many As, Bs, Cs, Ds, and Es you have and figure out where your boyfriend fits in. And from there, you'll know just what kinds of guests to expect.

(cont'd.)

QUIZ (cont'd.)

Mainly As:

Type: Frat-Party Boyfriend

Yes, it turns out your boyfriend likes to treat your shared apartment as his personal frat house. Generally, this means he enjoys throwing parties on a twenty-four-hour basis. It doesn't matter what day of the week it is, just as long as he can have his buddies over every single night until 3:00 AM.

How To Deal With It: Remind your boyfriend that you live in an apartment, not Studio 54. So if he wants to party nonstop, he needs to find a bar or club that will have him. Why? Because the bar may be open all hours, but your apartment is not. Make sure he knows it.

Mainly Bs:

Type: Gamer Boyfriend

Your boyfriend loves his video games. In fact, you know that when you come home from work or wake up in the morning, you'll find him sitting right in front of the TV playing *Halo*. This wouldn't be a problem, except usually his friends are sitting right along with him. Apparently, he's the only one in his crew with a gaming console—and they have to play somewhere, right?

How To Deal With It: First, let your boyfriend know that you completely understand his obsession. (After all, you did have a brief but passionate affair with Tetris back in the day.) So if he absolutely, positively has to play video games with his buds, then he should take his console to his friend's apartment. That way he *and* his friends can play video games whenever they like. And you won't have to hear the constant stream of button mashing.

(cont'd.)

QUIZ (cont'd.)

Mainly Cs:

Type: Sports-Nut Boyfriend

Your boyfriend is a jersey-wearing, Red Sox–loving sports fanatic. He loves sports so much that he's planning to name your first born LeBron. And according to him, watching sports with his buddies is a tradition. Besides, you two have a forty-two-inch flat-screen TV. There's no way he could watch the big game on his friend's twenty-six-inch tube. And to him, *every* game is the big game.

How To Deal With It: Admit that your boyfriend's right. You two do have a fabulous TV. But you know who has a better one? Hooters. And Hooters offers a two-for-one special on Thursday nights. Tell him to take his "tradition" there. And if he wants to bring you back some wings, you wouldn't complain.

Mainly Ds:

Type: Stoner Boyfriend

Your boyfriend has an obsession with a leafy illegal drug, and you're actually okay with it. What you're not okay with is his inviting his like-minded friends over to join him all the time. Apparently, toking up isn't fun unless it's a group effort.

How To Deal With It: Remind your boyfriend that you're a cool girlfriend. You're so cool that you're actually letting him partake in an illegal activity in your *shared* apartment—something that you *both* could get in trouble for. So if he needs to have a little reefer madness with a group of people, do it elsewhere. Namely, at one of his friend's apartments. At least there he won't get nagged about it.

(cont'd.)

QUIZ (cont'd.)

Mainly Es:

Type: Film-/Music-Geek Boyfriend

Your boyfriend knows everything there is to know about movies and/or music (especially genres you don't care about). He shares his hobby with a few of his closest friends. In fact, they love spending hours and hours watching cult classics and listening to Bob Dylan on vinyl in your living room. Why? Because your boyfriend has one of the best collections around. Lucky you.

How To Deal With It: Congratulate your boyfriend on spending years of his life building his massive library. He does have some good selections (such as *The Breakfast Club* and Madonna's *Like a Virgin* album). But do you know who else has a good movie selection? The multiplex down the block. And do you know where he could hear some really great music? At a concert. That's right. He has options other than your apartment. And if you're feeling up to it, you could join him, too.

✳   ✳   ✳   ✳   ✳   ✳   ✳   ✳   ✳   ✳

What if your boyfriend doesn't fall into any of those categories? Then stick to the basics. If he doesn't want to compromise on his "friend" time, then point out that you live in a *shared* apartment—not *his* apartment. So you both get to set the rules about who visits when.

◎ Visitation Rights

Your friends are good people (well, most of them). But just because they're good people doesn't mean they have good manners, which means you and your boyfriend need to discuss the house rules before your friends come over.

> ### Argument #1
> "You sound like a prison warden. You want me to have a set of house rules for my friends? I don't think so."

These rules aren't supposed to be like the Ten Commandments. You're not supposed to hand them out with the caveat, "Follow, or else God will smite you." No, that's too extreme—and weird. You just want these rules in place so you know what behavior is and isn't acceptable in your home.

For instance, if you're buying a nice, peacock silk carpet from the Pottery Barn, you may want to set up a "no shoes on the carpet" rule, because you don't want your guests tracking dirt all over it. If you're throwing a house-warming party, you may want to discuss whether or not to hide your best jewelry while people are over.

Moses forgot about these.

Sure, your friends are trustworthy, but what about the sketchy dates they may bring along?

These suggestions aren't intended to freak you out or get you to invest in a metal detector—no, no, no. They're just meant to get you thinking about what type of rules you want in place when your friends (or your boyfriend's friends) come for a visit. The questions below can help get you started:

- Smoking in the house. Allowed or not allowed?

- Friends with pets. Are you okay with your bestie bringing over her Chihuahua? What if her pet isn't house-trained?

- Bedroom locked or unlocked. Do you have friends who like to snoop? Do you even care?

- The borrowers. Is it okay for your friends to borrow your boyfriend's stuff (such as books, DVDs, deodorant, etc.) when he's not around?

- Video-game systems. Who can touch them and who can't?

- Shoes on or off when guests walk in the house?

- Are you a clean freak? Do you want to make sure your guests use napkins, plates, or lobster bibs?

- You break it, you buy it. If your boyfriend's buddy breaks your stuff, does he have to pay for it? Or can you just laugh off the fact he accidentally busted your custom-made, life-size Fabio statuette?

> **Argument #2**
>
> "Okay, those guidelines are all fine and dandy, but what happens if our friends don't follow them? Am I supposed to just kick them out?"

You're talking about *bad* friends. You know the ones (in fact, your boyfriend has a few of them). These are the friends who have no regard for your personal property. Maybe they've cracked your crystal china and refused to pay for it. Maybe they've borrowed your *Sex and the City* DVD set and claimed to have "lost" it. Or maybe they're just plain kleptomaniacs. How do you handle these people?

First, talk to your friends about how they're treating your apartment. Who knows, maybe they don't even realize how rude they're being. Most likely, once they get the scoop, they'll change their ways immediately. If they don't, then put your foot down and pull out a little Aretha Franklin, telling them they need to R-E-S-P-E-C-T your apartment. If they refuse, let them know they won't be allowed over again until they change their ways.

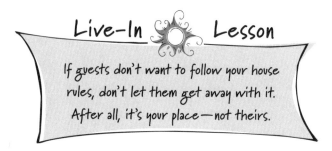

Live-In 🔆 Lesson

If guests don't want to follow your house rules, don't let them get away with it. After all, it's your place—not theirs.

◎ The Boarding House

At some point in your life, a family member, best friend, or random person you met at the dental convention will ask you for a favor: They will ask to stay at your apartment during a visit. If they're someone you actually want to see, you'll probably say, "Sure, why not? I'll break out the good sheets." Slow down there, Suzie Hospitality. Before you give that person the green light, you need to talk it over with your boyfriend first. It's his place, too, so he gets a say in who does and doesn't set up camp in your guest room.

While you're at it, discuss how long these out-of-towners can share your digs. Sure, you can handle Great-Aunt Zelda hanging around for one weekend, but what if she wants to stay longer? What if her vacation is open ended? It's best to know this information *before* a visitor arrives at your apartment, because the last thing you want is a houseguest who won't leave. You've seen those movies about houseguests from hell. Yes, they're hilarious (especially *Houseguest,* that one with Sinbad)—but that's only because you're not the one whose house it is.

Don't put yourself in that situation. Figure out a time limit that you and your boyfriend can agree on. If one week is your max and your friend wants to stay for three, then politely clue her in on your houseguest rules.

> **Argument**
> "Whoa, what if it's my future mother-in-law? You want me to tell her she can only stay with us for one week? That's not going to fly."

In cases like that, you don't have to be the bad guy. If it's your boyfriend's relative, former roommate, or some weirdo he met at a Foo Fighters concert, then he gets to be the lucky one to break the bad news. Sure, his guest may want to stay longer, but that doesn't matter. It's *your apartment.* You pay for it, so you get to set the rules. If your guests don't like it, point them to the Holiday Inn down the street, because that's where they'll be staying.

Now what about the in-town guests? You know the type—your boyfriend's buddy who lives five miles away but for some reason feels the need to crash at your place every other weekend. The guy who stays over so often that he has his own toothbrush holder. Look, you signed up to live with your boyfriend, not his friends. So if this situation is bothering you, discuss it with your boyfriend ASAP. When you do, your boyfriend will probably guilt trip you with the following:

- ⊛ "But his girlfriend kicked him out again. What was I supposed to do? Let him sleep on the street?"

- ⊛ "It's not his fault his place keeps getting set on fire—no one knows how to work those old ovens. Can't he stay for another night?"

- ⊛ "I know this is the third time he's been evicted, but his landlord is really out to get him."

Sometimes friends and family do fall on bad times, so you shouldn't turn your back on them in times of need. But if this is something that happens regularly, then stop feeling guilty. It's not your fault that your boyfriend's buddies (or whoever) don't have their act together. That's *their* fault. So let your boyfriend know he has two options: (a) Force his friends to sleep someplace else or (b) tell his friends they have to start paying rent. Why? Because sometimes the only way to get rid of a freeloader is to call their bluff. So do it.

Chapter Checklist

Expecting company? Keep these tips in mind:

- ☐ Decide how often your friends should be allowed over on a weekly basis. Don't freak out of it is not as often as you'd like. That's called compromise.

- ☐ Plan your house rules ahead of time. If your friends don't want to abide by them, hit the eject button.

- ☐ Decide how long and how often guests should be allowed to sleep over. Remember, you don't live at Freeloaders-R-Us.

10

Some Like It Hot

What's the best part about moving in with your boyfriend? You get to see him whenever you want. Feeling lonely? Guess what? You don't have to be, because your boyfriend is right there. Want to see the latest DiCaprio movie? No need to ask a friend to go with you, because you've already got a built-in movie buddy—your boyfriend. It's a pretty nice situation. And most likely, you two will get really comfortable together—so comfortable that you may start seeing your boyfriend as an on-call friend (with occasional X-rated benefits) rather than a live-in lover. When that happens, your romance-o-meter may go from hot to not.

ROMANCE-O-METER

I think the meter's broken.

What should you do in this situation? How do you bring the passion back into the bedroom? Act immediately. Buy some chocolate-covered strawberries, pull out your sexiest lingerie, and read this chapter.

It'll help you and your boyfriend break out of that relationship rut and spice up your love life in the process.

◎ Compliments Are a Girl's Best Friend

What's the simplest way to reignite your relationship? Compliments. That's right, a little positive feedback can go a long way. Think about it. How do you feel when your boyfriend randomly tells you how hot you look? Pretty tremendous, right? That's exactly why you need to do the same thing for him. If he's looking extra sexy in that tight blue T-shirt, let him know. If his hair is looking faboosh, point it out.

> **Argument**
> "What's the point in complimenting him? He already knows I think he's amazing."

Does he actually know that, or do you just *think* he knows that? Because sometimes when you've been in a relationship for a long time, you stop complimenting each other. You *assume* your boyfriend knows how great you think he is, just like you assume he knows to buy new toothpaste when the tube runs out. And what happens? You're the one who makes the midnight run to the drugstore for a fresh tube.

So stop making assumptions and start complimenting your boyfriend immediately—on his shoes, his cologne, his minty-fresh breath, whatever. If you wake up one Saturday morning and he miraculously decided to do the dishes *and* the laundry (yes, this would be a bizzaro universe), let him know he's your hero, because if you don't acknowledge these little things now, he'll begin to wonder why he's even trying. And eventually he'll start to feel underappreciated.

I learned this lesson firsthand. One evening my boyfriend sat down next to me and said, "You never compliment me anymore." I, of course, felt insulted, incredulous, and downright annoyed. After all, I complimented him all the time, and I told him that. He didn't believe me. In fact, he challenged me to name the last time I had. I rolled my eyes and thought...and thought. Eventually, I remembered the last time I complimented him—it had been *months* earlier.

Whenever my boyfriend had done something nice for me, I had acknowledged it—but only in my mind. Whenever he looked good, I noticed it—but I never mentioned it to him. That was the problem. I never let him know that I appreciated him or what he was doing for me. So he assumed that I didn't notice or just didn't care. That wasn't good for him or our relationship. So from that point on, I made an effort to break out the compliments—sometimes when he even deserved them.

Live-In Lesson

Make an effort to compliment your boyfriend. If you don't, he may start to feel
unhappy with you and your relationship.

◎ Date Night

"Date night." The term alone probably
makes you cringe and think:

- ◎ C'mon, I'm not my parents.
- ◎ We're *so* not at that level yet.
- ◎ Great, does that mean I should
  start planning for sex, too?

First off, don't knock date night.
Even though the concept may seem old-
fashioned (and desperate), it offers a lot of good benefits, the
main one being that you're forced to carve out some together
time with your boyfriend. You need this to give your relationship the love reboot it deserves, because most likely you
haven't been making time for your relationship. You've been
too busy with all the other things in your life: working, party
planning, or learning the art of origami.

Look, to have a healthy relationship, you have to work at it, which means you need to make time for it. Start by spending one night a week out with your boyfriend. That's right, a date night.

Argument

"Okay, I understand the gist of date night, but I don't need it. I live with my boyfriend, so every night is date night."

Yes, you and your boyfriend do spend most nights together, but do you actually engage in conversation? Or are you too busy watching trashy television shows, surfing online, or texting the latest gossip to your friends?

Live-In ☀ Lesson

Just because you're sitting next to your boyfriend doesn't mean you're spending time with him. It just means you're sharing space.

That's the point of date night—to keep that connection alive and extra spicy. So set aside a day once a week without your friends, your family, or your twin pugs. Plan a night for just you and your boyfriend. Maybe treat yourself to a fancy dinner or amp up the fun with a little activity, such as miniature golfing or shark diving. If money is tight, stay in and make lasagna together. Just figure out the best way to share some quality time.

If you want to keep date night interesting, then try something different once a month. Instead of going out to dinner, do something you've never done before. If you've always wanted to take a pottery class, drag your boyfriend along with you. If this sounds totally unsexy, rent the movie *Ghost* to see firsthand how Patrick Swayze and Demi Moore turn a pottery wheel into a tool for foreplay.

If pottery isn't for you, try traveling together. You don't have to go to an exotic country—the two of you can do something within driving distance. Go online to scope out any nearby attractions. Maybe a winery or a beach or an amusement park is located within a few hours of you. If that's too far to drive, check the newspaper for notices of any new art exhibits or bars opening around town.

Here's a little exercise for you and your boyfriend: Come up with a list of things you've always wanted to do but never had the chance. Maybe you want to explore a new hiking route, coffee shop, or wax museum. Whatever the ideas are, write each one on a separate slip of paper and put it into a jar.

Then once a month pick a slip of paper at random. Bam—that's your new activity for the month. Sometimes it'll be his idea, and sometimes it'll be yours. Either way, you'll be doing something different together, and that comfortable rut will be a thing of the past.

◎ Let's Talk about Sex

What's the best perk of a live-in relationship? Sex is at your disposal. That's right. No more driving across town to your boyfriend's apartment for a quickie. There's no need. You two live together now, so sex is only a bedroom (or kitchen floor) away. But now that you can have it whenever you want, you start putting it off. After all, it's not like the opportunity is going away, so you might as well fill your schedule with other things, right? And that's exactly what you start doing. You push sex to the bottom of your to-do list, until you eventually stop doing it altogether. This is what's known as a dry spell.

Argument #1

"We're not having a dry spell. We've just slowed down a bit. Besides, it's not like we can have sex twenty-four/seven. We do have lives outside the bedroom."

That's true. You can't have sex all the time, but that doesn't mean you should quit cold turkey. So what's stopping you? What's your reason for avoiding sex? Does it sound something like this?

Typical Reasons Why You Avoid Having Sex

- You feel bloated.
- Your cat doesn't like being left alone for too long.
- You have a headache.
- Your favorite reality show is on, and you want to see who gets voted off.
- You have to study for a test.
- You're too full from that giant cannoli you just ate.
- You want to wait until you're in a better mood.
- You just got a manicure.
- You just got a pedicure.
- You know it's your turn to be on top.

If you've used any of these excuses in the past, don't be ashamed. Just stop using them, because sex is too important to avoid. Not only is it pretty satisfying, it's also a bonding experience between you and your boyfriend. So if you're too tired, drink coffee. If you're too busy, clear your schedule. Just start making time for sex, even if it requires putting a reminder in your calendar. Yes, that takes away the spontaneity, but if that's what it takes to get you back in the bedroom, do it—for the both of you.

What if your reason for skipping sex runs a little bit deeper? What if you simply *don't like* having sex with your boyfriend? Ouch. That's a tough one, but you can deal with it. First, you have to figure out what the problem is: You're no longer attracted to your boyfriend (or vice versa), you're having bad sex, or the sex is just plain boring.

You're Not Attracted to Your Boyfriend Anymore

Your boyfriend has put on thirty-five pounds of relationship flab. And guess what? It just doesn't do it for you. In fact, it's a complete turnoff, which is why your sex life has gone from flying high to completely dry. How do you fix the problem? Well, you have two options. The first option is to accept it, because the longer you two are together, the more likely you'll both gain weight. (And let's be honest, who do you need to impress anymore?) So get used to your newly chunky-style boyfriend and learn to love him and his love handles.

The other option is to ask him to do something about the extra poundage. Just make sure to do this in a gentle fashion, because guys can be just as self-conscious about their bodies as girls. So start with a compliment. Let him know that you love him more than (insert the name of your celebrity crush or favorite department store). But you miss the way his body looked when you first got together. This may sound harsh, but, believe it or not, your boyfriend will appreciate your honesty. If he knows his jelly belly is the reason why your sex life has stalled, then he'll make a beeline to that ab machine, because he wants you to be attracted to him.

What if it's the opposite scenario? What if you're the one who's gained weight and now you're feeling totally unsexy? First off, talk to your boyfriend about it, because you may be delusional. Maybe you glimpsed yourself at a bad angle and assumed you were two sizes larger than what you actually are. If that's the case, get over the funhouse mirror image and start having sex with your boyfriend.

If you discover that you truly have put on some relationship flab, pull the workout gear out of the closet and start moving. Get yourself back to the way *you* want to look. Because if you don't feel good about yourself, then how do you expect anyone else to?

You're Having Bad Sex

If you're having bad sex, there's only one person to blame—yourself. Instead of telling your boyfriend there's a problem, you keep *hoping* that he'll figure it out on his own. That's like thinking if you wait long enough, the carpet will vacuum itself.

So stop the wishful thinking and tell your boyfriend exactly what you need. If you don't, he's never going to figure it out on his own. He'll just assume that you like everything he's been doing, because you've never told him otherwise.

Argument #2
"You want me to tell my boyfriend he sucks in the bedroom? Have you even been in a relationship before?"

Your boyfriend's number-one priority is to make you happy in bed. Seriously. He wants to be the top stud on your list of sex mates, and he'll do anything to make that happen. So be honest with him. If you're afraid you'll hurt his feelings, start by complimenting him on what he does well in the bedroom. And once you've won him over by praising his Don Juan status, politely let him know what you'd like him to do differently. Yes, this will be a little uncomfortable at first, but you'll both appreciate it in the long run.

The Sex Is Boring

That's right. Your sex life has become a snoozefest. It's really not surprising. The two of you have been having sex for a while now, so it has become routine. Tuesday is missionary night. Friday you're on top. Saturday and Sunday, well, you know the drill. And during the middle of these sexual exploits, your mind is elsewhere. You're:

- making a grocery list for tomorrow
- wondering who's going to be on Letterman tonight
- eating a sandwich
- inspecting your nails for any imperfections
- making shadow puppets on the wall

Yes, those are pretty clear signs that your sex life has become more boring than NPR during pledge week. So now's the time to spice things up and do something different. Maybe you need to try a new position, rent an X-rated movie, or buy a Catholic schoolgirl uniform and play teacher's pet. Just come up with some fresh new ideas that you'll both enjoy.

If you need some help, try the following activity. Create a list of all your sexual fantasies. Sure, you may have been too shy to vocalize them in the past, but

I can't wait to get my lips around that.

this time you're not saying them. You're writing them down on paper. So use your imagination. Have your boyfriend write up a fantasy list, too. Then swap lists and compare and contrast. If the two of you share any fantasies, start acting them out immediately. Then take turns playing out a fantasy on each other's list (as long as you're both comfortable doing it). When you're done with the original list, create more. And then more after that. Create as many lists as you need to keep your sex life alive and kicking.

> **Argument #3**
> "I hit the gym, bought lingerie, and even sent my boyfriend suggestive text messages. There's still nothing happening in the bedroom. Now what?"

Don't worry. Just because you're lost in the land of no sex doesn't mean you'll be stuck there forever. So start considering other options. Look into couple's therapy or talk to your doctor. After all, if you or your boyfriend's libido has gone from spicy to icy, then it could be symptomatic of a bigger issue. No matter the cause, seek out the help you need to flip that switch in the bedroom.

Chapter Checklist

Spice up your love life by reviewing the following items:

☐ Compliment your boyfriend (on his clothes, his hair, or his skills with a waffle iron). The more you do that, the more he'll appreciate you and your relationship.

☐ Date night is your friend, not your enemy. It helps keep you mentally engaged with your boyfriend, so schedule one at least once a week.

☐ Keep your sex life *muy caliente* by discussing what works and what doesn't work in the bedroom. Remember, a little conversation can go a long way.

Conclusion:
To Be or Not to Be?

*C*ongratulations! You've soldiered through all the chapters, taken all the quizzes, and passed with flying colors (or at least close to it). Now you're officially ready to move in with your boyfriend. Or, if you've already done that, you've learned how to work through all the kinks, the hard times, and the relationship ruts to keep your live-in situation running smoothly.

But what if you've shacked up and keep hitting roadblock after roadblock? What if all you see are "Hazardous Road Condition" signs ahead of you? Before you make that U-turn, take the quiz below. It'll help you determine whether your live-in is working or you've hit the point of no return.

✳ QUIZ: Is Your Live-in Relationship Working? ✳

1. Describe a typical night around the house together.
   a. Sitting on the couch and reading French poetry to each other.
   b. Watching TV in separate rooms—sorry, but I can't watch reruns of *Law & Order* anymore.

(cont'd.)

QUIZ (cont'd.)

   c. Me out with my friends and him out with his—in different places. Avoidance is key.

2. How do you deal with each other's dirty little bad habits?
   a. We try to accept them. After all, nobody's perfect.
   b. By quietly stewing and hoping that the bad habits will magically disappear.
   c. Yelling and screaming always seem like a good option.

3. Who handles the chores around the house?
   a. We both do. Cleaning together is fun!
   b. We usually share them, unless he has some work "emergency" to attend to, which is more often than not.
   c. He does. Sorry, not everything has to be equal.

4. Do you feel like your expenses are fairly distributed?
   a. Absolutely, although we've had to renegotiate a few times.
   b. For the most part, except when it comes to the groceries and magazine subscriptions. Seriously, why do I have to help pay for *Sports Illustrated*?
   c. Nope, and he refuses to discuss it.

5. How do you handle a disagreement?
   a. Talk, talk, and then talk some more.
   b. We don't. We pretend like it didn't happen.
   c. With mean looks, followed by random digs at each other's character. Is that so wrong?

6. How often do you argue?
   a. Maybe once a month. What's there to fight about?

(cont'd.)

QUIZ (cont'd.)

    b. Once or twice a week. Is it so hard for him to put his Mr. T coffee mug in the dishwasher?

    c. Every single day. How else are we supposed to communicate?

7. Do you regret moving in together?

    a. No way, best decision of my life.

    b. Sometimes, but only after we have a bad argument.

    c. Every second of every day, but that's normal, right?

Now count up how many As, Bs, and Cs you have. Check the results below to find out what it means about your relationship.

Mainly As: Lucky you! It sounds like your live-in relationship is right on track. You're still laughing, smiling, and genuinely enjoying each other's company. If you have a disagreement, you talk it out. If something isn't working, you figure out a way to compromise. That's exactly how any good cohabitation should be, so pat yourself on the back. You're still in it to win it.

But remember, just because your live-in situation is running smoothly now doesn't mean you can neglect it. So put your game face on and keep at it.

Mainly Bs: Living together is not all rainbows and sunny days anymore. Instead, you're living in overcast city and starting to have serious doubts about your cohabitation. Maybe it's because you and your boyfriend can't seem to agree on anything. Or maybe you've discovered that his dirty little bad habit is really a deal breaker (or vice versa). Or maybe your lovey-dovey idea of a live-in relationship isn't remotely close to reality.

(cont'd.)

QUIZ (cont'd.)

Either way, don't give up the fight. Yes, it's a struggle and at times more painful than a root canal, but that's okay. Cohabitation is a new thing for both of you, so of course you're going to take some missteps along the way. So figure out what changes are needed to make you both happy and then start adjusting immediately. Trust me, it's worth the extra effort.

Mainly Cs: You've checked out of your relationship. You can't stand your boyfriend's face, his voice, or his musky odor (and he feels the same way about you). In fact, you two have officially become Michael Douglas and Kathleen Turner in *War of the Roses*—miserable and ready to tear your live-in relationship to pieces.

Before you start throwing furniture at each other, think about whether you've given your live-in a fighting chance. If it has only been a few months, then you may still be in the adjustment phase (or, as I like to call it, the "is-he-really-worth-losing-sleep-and-closet-space-over?" phase). Wait until you're past this point before you even think about calling it quits.

If you've already moved beyond it, ask yourself a few questions. Have you compromised? Have you sought out couples' therapy? Have you two truly talked things out (and no, hurling insults does not count as talking)? If so (and if you're both still unhappy), it may be time to reassess your relationship, or even end it. Not all live-ins are meant to be. And, unfortunately, yours may be one of them.

So how did you do? Win, lose, or draw? Whatever the outcome is, remember, even the best live-in relationships can hit rough patches. The keys to getting through it are practice, patience, and perseverance. So if you ever lose your footing, need a quick pick-me-up, or want advice about a relationship meltdown, this book is here for you.

Times may get rough. But in the end, a live-in relationship is well worth the effort. So live it, love it, and learn from it. Good luck!